Elevating Child Care

A GUIDE TO RESPECTFUL PARENTING

Janet Lansbury

Janet Lansbury

Elevating Child Care: A Guide to Respectful Parenting
Copyright (c) 2014 by Janet Lansbury

ISBN: 978-1499103670

Published by JLML Press, 2014

All identifying details, including names, have been changed
except for those pertaining to the author's family members.
Material contained in this book is available on the author's
website. This book is not intended as a substitute for advice
from a licensed professional.

~

Cover Photo and Design: Sara Prince
www.bonzochoochmushyandme.com

For more information about the author, please visit her
website at: www.JanetLansbury.com.

TABLE OF CONTENTS

Introduction

Finding a Passion for Parenting

Parenting is one of life's most fulfilling experiences. It can also be exhausting, frustrating, and utterly confounding.

The difficulties I faced as a new mother caught me off guard. I had looked forward to motherhood all my life and assumed that caring for a baby would happen naturally. Instead, I soon found that I had no clue.

My baby was adorable, yet never in my life had I felt so tired, lost, inept and disappointed in myself. The mothering instincts I had assumed would provide me with clarity and guidance never materialized. My life had become a monotonous succession of feeding, burping, diapering, entertaining, and soothing tears (lots and lots of tears, most of them my daughter's). Though I combed desperately through stacks of popular parenting books, I found nothing that resonated.

At my wits end, I fatefully stumbled upon RIE (Resources for Infant Educators), the respectful approach to parenting founded by infant specialist and child care pioneer Magda Gerber. The approach made immediate sense to me, and I embraced it like a drowning victim with a life preserver.

Before long I had experienced a radical transformation in both perception and experience: first, by discovering my baby's astounding natural abilities to learn *without* being taught, to develop motor and cognitive skills, communicate, face age appropriate struggles, initiate and direct independent play for extended periods and much more; then by realizing the tremendous energy and stress I had been wasting by struggling to entertain and second-guess my child.

Over the years, Magda became my dear friend and mentor, and her philosophy of child care my passion. I became a RIE parenting teacher, a lecturer at Early Childhood conferences, an active blogger with millions of readers worldwide, a personal parenting consultant, and an author.

This book is a collection of 30 popular and widely read articles from my website. They focus on some of the most common aspects of infant and toddler child care and how respectful parenting can be applied.

You will find Magda's name or a quote from her on nearly every page of this book. Everything I know and write about springs from her wisdom and my own experience – with the hundreds of infants and toddlers who have come through my classes, and with my own three children (now 21, 17 and 12).

RIE parenting can be summed up as an *awareness* of our baby's perspective. We perceive and acknowledge our infants to be unique, separate people. We enhance our awareness by observing them — allowing them the bit of space they need to show us who they are and what they need.

RIE parenting also makes us more self-aware. Through our sensitive observations we learn not to jump to conclusions; for example, that our babies are bored, tired, cold, hungry, or want to hold the toy they seem to notice across the room.

We learn not to assume that grumbling or fussing means babies need to be propped to sitting, picked up, or rocked or bounced to sleep. We recognize that, like us, babies sometimes have feelings that they want to share and will work through them in their own way with our support.

We learn to differentiate our children's signals from our own projections. We become more aware of the habits we create (like sitting babies up or jiggling them to sleep), habits that can then become our child's needs. These are artificially created needs rather than organic ones.

In short, RIE parenting asks us to use our minds as well as our instinct, to look and listen closely and carefully before we respond.

Sensitive observation proves to us that our babies are competent individuals with thoughts, wishes and needs of their own. Once we discover this truth there's no turning back. Then, like Alison Gopnik, one of several psychologists on the forefront of an exciting new wave of infant brain research, we might wonder: *"Why were we so wrong about babies for so long?"*

Practiced observers like Magda Gerber were *not* wrong. More than sixty years ago, she and her mentor, pediatrician Emmi Pikler, knew what Gopnik's research is finally now proving: infants are born with phenomenal learning abilities, unique gifts, deep thoughts and emotions. Pikler and Gerber dismissed the notion of babies as "cute blobs" and understood them as whole people deserving of our respect.

Magda's RIE approach can perhaps be best described as putting respect for babies into action. Here's how:

1. We communicate authentically. We speak in our authentic voices (though a bit more slowly with babies and toddlers), use real words and talk about real things, especially things that directly pertain to our babies and things that are happening *now*.

2. We encourage babies to build communication skills by asking them questions, affording them plenty of time to respond, always acknowledging their communication.

3. We invite babies to actively participate in care giving activities like diapering, bathing, meals and bedtime rituals and give them our full attention during these activities. This inclusion and focused attention nurtures our parent-child relationship, providing children the sense of security they need to be able to separate and engage in self-directed play.

4. We encourage uninterrupted, self-directed play by offering even the youngest infants free play opportunities, sensitively observing so as not to needlessly interrupt, and trusting that our child's play choices are *enough*. Perfect, actually.

5. We allow children to develop motor and cognitive skills naturally according to their innate timetables by offering them free play and movement opportunities in an enriching environment, rather than teaching, restricting or otherwise interfering with these organic processes. Our role in development is primarily *trust.*

6. We value intrinsic motivation and inner-directedness, so we acknowledge effort and take care not to over-praise. We trust our children to know themselves better than we know them, so we allow children to lead when they play and choose enrichment activities, rather than projecting our own interests.

7. We encourage children to express their emotions by openly accepting and acknowledging them.

8. We recognize that children need confident, empathetic leaders and clear boundaries -- but not shaming, distractions, punishments or time out.

9. We allow our children to problem solve, experience and learn from age-appropriate conflicts with our support.

10. We understand the power of our modeling and recognize that our children are learning from us through our every word and action about love, relationships, empathy, generosity, gratitude, patience, tolerance, kindness, honesty and respect. Most profoundly, they're learning about themselves, their abilities, their worth, and their place in our hearts and in the world.

What I am most grateful to Magda Gerber and RIE for is the deeply trusting, mutually respectful relationships I have with my own children. Respect and trust have a boomerang effect -- they come right back at you. As Magda promised me would happen, I've raised kids I not only love, but "in whose company I love being."

Magda died in 2007, well into her 90's. I think about her every day, and she continues to inspire my life and work. I miss her.

1.

What Your Baby Can't Tell You
(In The Beginning)

Years ago, I had a major awakening. It hit me that my three-month-old baby was an actual person. I had brought her to a RIE parenting class and was asked to place her on her back on a blanket next to me. She lay there for two hours — peaceful, alert, engaged, and self-contained. She didn't make a sound, but I felt the power of her presence, a self-assuredness that at age 21 still knocks my socks off.

What I observed in that parenting class for the first time was not just my baby — it was a whole person with her own mind, a mind I wanted to become intimately acquainted with, and human needs no different than yours or mine. Maybe other parents figure this out right away, but I didn't.

Without that moment of clarity, I'm not sure when I would have seen beyond the needy infant to the person — possibly not until she began walking, saying recognizable words, or at least communicating to me by pointing or gesturing. Intellectually, I knew she was all there, but not to the extent that I would think to put myself in her shoes (or booties) and treat her in the way I would wish to be treated.

One of the most profound lessons I've learned since becoming a mom -- reinforced by observing hundreds of other parents and babies interact — is that there is a self-fulfilling prophecy to the way we view our babies: If we believe them to be helpless, dependent, needy (albeit lovely) creatures, their behavior will confirm those beliefs.

Alternatively, if we see our infants as capable, intelligent, responsive people ready to participate in life, initiate activity, receive and return our efforts to communicate with them, then we find that they are all of those things.

I am not suggesting that we treat infants as small adults. They need a baby's life, but they deserve the same level of human respect that we give to adults. Here are some examples of baby care that reflect the way I like to be treated:

Tell me what's going on. If I had a stroke that made me as dependent as an infant -- meaning that I couldn't take care of my own needs or express myself -- I would hope to be warned before I was being touched, lifted, fed, sponged, rinsed, dressed, given a shot, etc. I would want to know everything that was going on in my immediate world, especially if it directly related to my body. I would want to be invited to participate to the extent I was capable (i.e., given an opportunity to hold the spoon myself).

At first it feels awkward talking to someone who does not talk back, but we quickly get used to it. Babies begin to understand our respectful intention to include them much earlier than we might believe. And they communicate earlier if we open the door.

Give me attention. Babies need undivided attention

from loved ones, just like you and I do, especially when we are joined physically (as in breastfeeding). Several minutes of real attention in intervals each day is more fulfilling than hours and hours of empty physical contact. Sitting in the car next to my husband while he talks on the phone for an extended period of time makes me feel invisible – certainly not important, loved or appreciated.

When someone touches me, especially when it's intimate (as in a baby's doctor appointment, bath or diaper change), I want to be included in what is going on, encouraged to pay attention, not asked to look elsewhere and ignore what's happening.

Hear me, don't just fix me. Relationship counselors teach it, and it applies to our babies, too. I want my feelings heard, not fixed. Please don't 'shush' and pacify all my cries, sticking something in my mouth just to stop my tears. I want to be able to try to tell you what I need before you assume it. Sometimes I just want to cry in your arms and have it be okay with you. Relax. It feels comforting to have you here, calmly listening and trying to understand.

Let me create and initiate my own activities. I like tagging along on adventures with the people I love sometimes, but I also crave time to initiate activity that I choose. Give me a quiet, safe place where I am not hemmed in, so I can move my body and have uninterrupted thoughts and daydreams. I need time to figure out the way my marvelous hands work, and why there are things like breezes that I feel but cannot see.

What I'm doing may not look like much, but I'm actually very busy. (And when I am deeply involved in something, please don't interrupt me to change my diaper.)

I love knowing that you are nearby in case I need you, or within shouting distance, but please don't get me in the habit of following you all the time when there is so much I could be experiencing for myself.

Notice the things I like to do. Let me show you the interesting person I am.

Trust me with the truth. You don't have to smile at me when you're upset. Be honest with me. Be yourself, so that I can be myself, too. We have lots to learn about each other. It won't always be perfect together, but it will be real. And when you are worrying and projecting about the future, I'll tug you back into the moment. Promise.

2.

Connecting With Your Kids

I have a keen interest in every aspect of child care, but the advice I share is focused on one goal: Building healthy relationships with our kids.

There's a lot riding on this. The quality of our connection will dictate whether teaching our children appropriate behavior is simple and successful, or whether it is confusing, discouraging and ineffective. It will decide whether our children feel secure and retain the sure sense of self and confidence that helps them fulfill their potential. And perhaps most importantly: Our relationship will be forever embedded in our child's psyche as her model of love and the ideal she'll seek for future intimate bonds.

In the impressionable first years especially, every interaction we have with our children is an opportunity to deepen our connection... or not. Sometimes a missed connection is just a minor wasted opportunity. In other instances, missed connections create distance, lessen trust, and are even invalidating for our children.

Connecting often means overriding our instincts and emotional impulses and thinking before we act. Here are some common examples:

We don't want to hear crying. Hearing and acknowledging our children's emotions can be intensely challenging, but it is essential for raising healthy children who feel connected to us.

We disconnect when we discount their feelings ("Oh, don't be frightened, it's only a puppy"), or invalidate ("That didn't really hurt" or "Those aren't real tears"), or rush feelings through ("Okay, okay, that's enough now"), or when we misread our infant or toddler's cries and try to calm her before listening and understanding.

Since feelings are involuntary (and even if they seem forced, who are we to decide this?), these disconnected responses also teach children that they aren't wholly acceptable to their loved ones, that they can't trust themselves or their feelings.

The secret to connecting is to meet children where they are. Listen patiently and acknowledge. We can never go wrong or overboard when we acknowledge: "You are so upset we have to leave. Oh, this is terribly upsetting for you! I said we had to go when you really, really wanted to stay longer. You were having so much fun!"

We don't want to be the bad guy. Distraction is the polar opposite of connection, yet I often hear it advised as an acceptable "redirection" tool for infants and toddlers.

Distraction doesn't teach appropriate behavior. What it does teach children is that they don't rate an honest connection in their first and most formative years. So these distractions, along with other manipulative, controlling methods like bribes, tricks and (most disconnecting of all) punishments threaten the relationship of trust necessary for close parent-child bonds.

Children need simple, truthful, empathetic, but direct responses, especially when they are testing and learning limits. The parent who confronts situations honestly, acknowledging the child's point of view and possible (more like probable) displeasure may worry about being the bad guy, but this will be the "trusted", genuine guy, the brave person the child feels closest to and safest with.

We get invested in what our child plays or learns.

"Wouldn't life be easier for both parents and infants if parents would observe, relax and enjoy what their child is doing, rather than keep teaching what the child is not yet capable of?"

– Magda Gerber

Trusting your child, appreciating what he or she is doing *right now*, will bond you and transmit positive messages of acceptance and appreciation to your child.

Again, the key is to meet children where they are. The way children choose to play and learn is usually better than enough – it is the perfect thing for them to be doing at that particular time.

My own son's birthday party several years ago was yet another great reminder of the power of ditching agendas and valuing what *is*. We'd spent the afternoon decorating our house with cobwebs, ghosts and other scary things at our son's request and a dear friend, our son's beloved godfather, had been handling DJ duties.

We were all set for a house party, but our son and his guests had another plan. They took the glow stick party favors outdoors and spent the entire evening exuberantly throwing them at each other under the moonlight, a game they invented called "Rainbow Wars".

To another family, this might have been disappointing, but we were amused and totally thrilled about the great time the kids were having. We've since celebrated this success together.

We don't have patience for exaggerated, over-dramatic, unreasonable behavior. Toddlers can seem to have overblown reactions, emotions and behaviors. They can seem to be greedy, self-centered, oversensitive, cry babies, braggarts, and the list goes on. It's as if toddlers are unconsciously auditioning annoying behaviors just to test our reaction. Will we be accepting, understanding, on their team? They need us to be.

I admire one of the parents I work with so much for realizing she needs help with this. She has a tendency (passed down to her from her own parents) to discount her daughter's point of view. She feels herself 'going there' almost against her will. For example, if her daughter complains that another child bumped into her and her mom sees that it's obviously nothing serious, she might reflexively say, "Oh, he didn't mean to. It's fine."

I'm encouraging her to try to catch herself before she does this and instead meet her child where she is by acknowledging her perspective. "Oh, did that hurt you? Sorry to hear that. You and Peter bumped into each other? Ouch!" Subtle adjustments like these are the difference between connecting and invalidating.

We want to get care-giving duties over with. Diapering, feeding, bathing and bedtime are important opportunities to slow down and connect. We do that by paying attention and inviting children to participate, even when it's not going well — especially when it's not going well. These activities are prime time for the kind of intimacy that not only deepens our connection, but also refuels our child's body and soul.

I'm often asked, "How can I pay attention when the baby needs to feed 24/7?" Or, "But my toddler hates having his diaper changed. I have to distract him and get it over with quickly." Ironically, these are common results of disconnection. Babies need to nurse less and appreciate diapering more when we are engaged during these activities.

"Whenever you care, do it absolutely with full attention. If you pay half attention all the time, that's never full attention. Babies are then always half hungry for attention."
- Magda Gerber

We hesitate to express love, appreciation, gratitude or apologies because our child doesn't seem to be listening. Whether our children are infants, toddlers, teens or somewhere in between, when we talk about the feelings that connect us, they're listening.

One of my RIE Parent-Infant Guidance Classes met for the last time recently, and I bid farewell to families I'd sat on the floor with each week for almost two years. I started sharing with two-year-old Maren -- strong, sweet and sometimes feisty -- how much I had enjoyed watching her grow and play. She walked away. I continued. The moment I finished she turned around and surprised me with the most tender hug and kiss.

3.

The Key to Your Child's Heart

Write this word on your hand: **Acknowledge.**

It's a magical way to connect with a child of any age. Acknowledge your child's feelings and wishes, even if they seem ridiculous, irrational, self-centered or wrong. It can ease tears and tantrums, and even prevent them. It's a simple but surprisingly challenging thing to do, particularly in the heat the moment.

Acknowledgement isn't agreeing with or condoning our child's actions; it's validating the feelings behind them. It's a simple, profound way to reflect our child's experience and inner self. It demonstrates our understanding and acceptance. It sends a powerful, affirming message: Every thought, desire, feeling – every expression of our mind, body and heart – is perfectly acceptable, appropriate and lovable.

Acknowledging is simple, but it isn't easy. It's counter-intuitive for most of us, even when we've done it thousands of times.

Won't acknowledging our child's wishes make matters worse? Won't saying, "I know how much you want an ice cream cone like he one your friend has, and it does look yummy, but we won't be having dessert until later" make our toddler hold on to the idea longer, cry harder? Wouldn't it be better to dismiss or downplay the child's feelings, distract, redirect or say,"Oh, sweetie, not now"?

Our fears about an honest acknowledgement of the situation are almost always unfounded. Feeling heard and understood allows children to release the feelings, let go and move on.

Here are more reasons that acknowledging our child's truth is worth the conscious effort it takes:

Acknowledging can stop tears and tantrums. I have witnessed this many, many times. Whether a child is upset about an injury, a disagreement with another child, or angry over a conflict with a parent, acknowledging to the child what happened or that he is hurt, frustrated or angry can miraculously ease the pain. Feeling understood is a powerful thing.

Acknowledging, instead of judging or "fixing", fosters trust and encourages children to keep sharing their feelings. Parents and caregivers have an enormous influence, and their responses have an impact on young children. If, for example, we try to calm children by assuring them that there's no need to be upset or worried about something that's troubling them, they may become less inclined to express their feelings. If our goal is our child's emotional health and keeping the door of communication open – just acknowledging is the best policy. "Daddy left and you are sad."

I was reminded of this recently when one of my teenage daughters shared her anger and heartbreak over a long time best friend's lies and betrayal. How hard it was not tell her that this friend is flawed and that my daughter deserves so much better! How hard it was to just listen and acknowledge the hurt and disappointment.

As painful as this experience was for me, I treasure it, because my daughter trusted me with her innermost feelings. I'll do all in my power to encourage her to share with me again. (My daughter ended up resuming her relationship with her long adored friend, having noted her limitations, and I was so glad I held my tongue.)

Acknowledging informs a child's emotional intelligence and encourages language development. Children gain clarity about their feelings and desires when we verbally reflect them. *But don't state the feeling unless you're sure.* It's safer to use the words "upset" or "bothered" rather than jumping to "scared", "angry", etc.

When in doubt, you might ask, "Did it make you mad when Joey wouldn't let you use his blocks?" "Did the dog's bark frighten you or just surprise you?"

Talking to babies, toddlers, children of all ages about these real things happening to them is the most powerful, meaningful and natural way for them to learn language.

Acknowledging illuminates – helps us understand and empathize. To state our child's point of view, we have to first see it, so acknowledging helps to give us clarity. When we say, "You want me to keep playing this fun game with you, but I'm too tired", we are encouraged to empathize with our child's point-of-view (and he ours).

Acknowledging the situation and asking questions (especially when we don't know the reason our child is upset) can help us unravel the mystery. "You're upset and look uncomfortable. You just ate, your diaper is dry. Maybe you need to burp? Okay, I'm going to pick you up."

Acknowledging struggles might be all the encouragement your child needs to carry on. This is another scenario in which a simple acknowledgement can work like magic. Rather than saying, "You can do it," which can create pressure and set the child up to believe he disappoints us, try saying, "You are working very hard, and you're making progress. That is tough to do. It's frustrating, isn't it?"

Acknowledging instead of praising helps children stay inner-directed. This is as simple as containing our impulse to cheer loudly or say "good job!", and instead smiling and reflecting, "You pulled the plastic beads apart. That was really hard."

"Let your child's inner joy be self-motivating. You can smile and express your genuine feelings but should refrain from giving excessive compliments, clapping your hands, and making a big fuss. If you do this, your child starts seeking satisfaction from external sources. She can get hooked on praise, becoming a performer seeking applause instead of an explorer. Praise also disrupts and interrupts a child's learning process. She stops what she's doing and focuses on you, sometimes not returning to the activity."
– Magda Gerber, *Your Self-Confident Baby*

Acknowledging proves that we are paying attention, makes a child feel understood, accepted,

deeply loved and supported. Could there be any better reason to give it a try?

> *"People will forget what you said; people will forget what you did, but people will never forget how you made them feel."*
> -Maya Angelou

> *"We all need someone who understands."*
> - Magda Gerber

4.

How to Love a Diaper Change

Call me sensitive, but I once saw a diaper change that made me cry. In fact, I can tear up just thinking about it.

It was a scene from a film about the The Pikler Institute, the highly respected orphanage in Budapest, Hungary, founded by pediatrician and infant expert Dr. Emmi Pikler. The camera focuses on a 3-week-old new arrival being welcomed with a diaper change. We hear the caregiver speaking slowly and see her gentle touches. The subtitles read: "Now I will lift your legs. I will move the diaper under you." She pauses after she explains each action, giving the infant a few moments to respond and anticipate what will happen next.

Several minutes later, the delicate task completed, the caregiver says quietly to the tiny, trusting person: "I think you will like it here."

Diaper changes are built for intimacy. All we need to turn diapering from a difficult, dreaded chore into a mutually gratifying experience is to change our perception -- to appreciate the moment as an opportunity for developing a closer partnership with our child.

Remembering to slow down, to include our baby instead of distracting him, ask for his assistance, use gentle "asking hands" instead of busy, efficient ones can literally transform a mundane task into a time of mutual enrichment.

It will not always be easy. Toddlers test, and that's exactly what they are supposed to do. A toddler has failed if he makes life too easy for us.

Here are some ideas for making the most of diaper changes with our infants and toddlers:

Set the tone with a respectful beginning. I'm amazed when parents stop a child in his tracks to open the back of his pants, or say, "Ew, smelly! Someone needs a diaper change!" It's all I can do to refrain from asking, "Would you like to be treated that way? If you passed gas in public would we be waving our hands, holding our noses and grabbing at your pants?"

Children don't like to be interrupted when they are playing, and most diaper changes can be postponed until there is a lull in an infant or toddler's activity.

Wait for a break in your child's play and then say discreetly, "Please let me check your diaper now". Then, "We're going to change your diaper." If the child walks, you might give the option, "Would you like to walk to the changing table or shall I carry you?"

If he resists, you may be able to give him the choice of a bit more time. "I see you're still playing. In five minutes we will change your diaper." Toddlers crave autonomy and are more amenable to cooperation when we respect their need to make some decisions.

Give undivided, unplugged attention. Embrace this time together, and your baby will, too. Release yourself from other concerns to focus for these few minutes on your child. *Slow down.* Even the youngest infants sense our hurry or distraction, and it makes them tense and resistant, rather than willing participants. Our slow, gentle touch breeds trust.

If the child seems distracted, acknowledge it and wait. "You hear that loud siren. I hear it, too. Now, it seems to have passed. Are you ready for me to unsnap your pajama?" Or, "You're crying. Did I lie you down too quickly? Do you need me to hold you for a moment before we start?"

Remind yourself to pay attention to the whole person, not just his lower half. Don't do anything without telling him first. Not only are we treating him with respect by telling him what is happening, we are encouraging him to absorb language with all his senses (the cold wipes, the sound of the snaps on his pajamas).

Ask for your baby's assistance. You will find joy in your baby's responsiveness. He soon shows you he can place his hands through a sleeve; contract his abdominal muscles to help you lift his bottom; hold the diaper and the diaper cream.

When diapering time is finished we ask, "Are you ready for me to pick you up?" Our baby will learn to extend his arms to us in reply. Surprisingly, even the youngest infants respond when we ask to pick them up by preparing their muscles for a change in altitude and position.

Be flexible. Stay open to new possibilities. When infants become mobile, they need us to adjust to their needs as best we can. A baby might wish to roll to his tummy to be wiped, or be in an all fours crawling position. The toddler may need to stand and be changed on a pad on the floor. Continue to ask for cooperation, but compromise and allow the child to do things his way if you can make it work.

Imagine new ways your child might be able to be more participatory. Invite him to wipe himself, put on his own cream, and take his diaper on or off. Children of all ages want to be trusted to do things for themselves whenever possible. If you keep your mind open to all the possibilities, you will be surprised by all your baby can do.

Remember, your goal is partnership. Are all diaper changes smooth and easy? No way! A securely attached child tests us…often.

Sometimes we start off on the wrong foot, the baby is too tired (or we are) and the whole thing is a disastrous mess. Forget about feeling connected — we may not even particularly like our baby in that moment. These are normal bumps in the road. Best to embrace those, too, and acknowledge to our child, "Wow, that was a tough one, wasn't it?"

As Ruth Anne Hammond explains in her insightful book, *Respecting Babies: A New Look At Magda Gerber's RIE Approach*: "If [a parent] is usually slow, gentle, and attentive, an occasional lapse is emotionally manageable for the child, and may even be helpful in the process of learning that her parent is human."

Diapering is not just about getting a job done or having a clean baby. Our hands are a baby's introduction to the world. If they touch slowly, gently, and "ask" a child for cooperation rather than demand it, we are rewarded with a relationship bound in trust, respect and the inexorable knowledge of our importance to each other.

"One generally finds that infants are the most content and cheerful in the hands of mothers who move with ceremonious slowness."

–Dr. Emmi Pikler

5.

Good Grief

Loren needed to leave the parenting class to make a phone call. She walked with trepidation toward the door, but then she paused and asked me, "Should I just go?" Since she had clearly told her ten-month-old Trevor what she was doing, I encouraged her, "Yes!" Seeing his mother depart, Trevor began to cry. I approached him and spoke softly. "Your mom went out. She's coming back. You didn't want her to go."

The simple acknowledgement of Trevor's point of view calmed him almost instantly. He sniffled once or twice and then sat patiently, eyes fixed on the door, waiting for his mom to return.

This situation was repeated the following week in class. Loren told Trevor, "I'm going to the bathroom," and somewhat tentatively walked out. Trevor cried. I went to him and said, "You didn't want her to go. She's coming back. It's hard when your mom leaves and you don't want her to. Do you want me to pick you up?" (He didn't.) This time Trevor continued to cry for a seemingly endless minute. I felt the discomfort of everyone in the class, including my own! Finally, having expressed his pain completely, he became quiet, sat still for a moment, then reached for a nearby ball.

By the time Loren came back he was involved in play, but when he saw her he cried out to her and seemed to be objecting to her previous action. She sat with him and allowed him to finish his complaints. He soon became interested in his surroundings again.

No one likes to hear the sound of a crying baby. Even a few seconds of crying can be unbearable for most adults to hear. Whether we are a parent, grandparent or paid caregiver, we feel that we are failing if the child in our care is upset. We want to distract a crying child, to make the child smile, and we will do almost anything in our power to put an end to the feeling that is triggering the child's tears. But ask yourself: When a loved one leaves, should we not feel a sense of loss and sadness?

Let's say we follow our natural urges when dealing with Trevor. When Trevor's mom leaves, he cries, we rush to him. "It's okay, it's okay! Mommy's coming back! Don't cry…shhhh shhhh. Oh, look at this ball…here, catch it, catch it! Yay!"

This action could indeed put an abrupt end to Trevor's outburst and he would stop crying. But what is the child learning? Most importantly, where did those feelings of loss go?

Fast-forward a few years. Trevor's beloved family dog dies. His parents are devastated and Trevor's sad cries only magnify their grief. "Trevor…Oh, it's okay, it's okay! Don't cry…shhhh! It's all right. We have to be strong. We'll get another dog—a new puppy!"

The recent death of my mother has given me renewed interest in the grief process. The problem, as so aptly put by John W. James and Russell Friedman in *The Grief Recovery Handbook,* is that, "We're taught how to acquire things, not what to do when we lose them." Parents, friends, and even society encourage us to cover up grief rather than to deal with it productively: Don't feel bad. Replace the loss. Be strong for others. Keep busy.

These are a sampling of the spoken and unspoken suggestions we are given, starting at a young age, for dealing with grief. They require us to ignore our honest feelings, hold them in, bury them. They are well-intentioned ideas sprung from the discomfort of those around us; no one wants to see us upset. But these directions only undermine our ability to express our true feelings, steering us to the incomplete resolution of grief and loss.

Grieving people want and need to be heard, not fixed. But grievers also want the approval of others, and thus feel the need to appear recovered for them. Our suppressed and unresolved feelings will then diminish our *joie de vivre* and sap our life energy. We may seek relief in drugs, alcohol, or other addictive behaviors. At best, we are responding unnaturally to loss and disappointment, continuing habits that threaten future happiness and a sense of well being. This is why it is vital to learn how to cope with loss in its simplest and earliest forms.

At RIE we are fortunate to study emotional health at the beginning of life, and as I pondered the origins of grief for a child, I thought of infants like Trevor experiencing the momentary absence of a loved one. A parent's separation, even to go into the next room, is indeed the first loss most children face. If we can handle this situation carefully, perhaps we can send a child in a healthy direction as they experience future losses in life.

Another early loss children deal with occurs when a sibling is born. The older child's relationship with his primary caregivers is altered suddenly and profoundly. No matter how sensitively the parents handle the situation, no matter how much the child appears to 'love' the new baby, there is grief for the pre-existing situation, for what once was. The new third party causes forced reconfiguration of the child's place in his world and tremendous loss. If a child can be trusted and encouraged to express the gamut of negative feelings he or she may be having, and if parents can use what energy they have to keep behavioral limits consistently intact while allowing for painful feelings, then the child can stay on the course of healthy emotional release.

When the children in our care are grieving a loss, no matter how insignificant the loss may seem to us, our job is to facilitate that loss and simply let them grieve. Magda Gerber often reminded her students, "Sometimes we win, sometimes we lose."

Trevor, and all infants, can be trusted to grieve as an individual in a unique and perfect way. Infants demonstrate the authentic expression of their feelings when given the opportunity. If we can give them the space and time to express painful feelings instead of arresting their cries, and if we can steady ourselves to work through our own discomfort, then our children can be reassured that their true responses are accepted and appropriate.

Children thus can continue to experience loss naturally, learn to deal with loss capably, and know that loss is survivable. This mindful approach is vital because when we adopt it, far from failing, we are providing the highest level of care...and love.

6.

Babies and Sleep

"The word 'sleep' wakes up even the sleepiest baby."
— Magda Gerber

Magda Gerber's assertion might seem far-fetched, but recent scientific studies (by Gopnik, Bloom, Spelke and others) are proving what Gerber understood more than half a century ago: our infants are astonishingly sharp and aware. They recognize repeated words, read our subtexts, sense our feelings and attitudes.

Through my decades observing infants and toddlers, I've noted that they are even inclined to resist anything they perceive to be our agenda, especially if they sense us selling it to them.

Magda recommended replacing 'sleep' with 'rest', partly because rest is a little gentler, less demanding. Also, for many of us, sleep can have a vaguely negative connotation, which we can end up inadvertently conveying to our children.

Consider two of the phrasings we most commonly use like "go to sleep", which sounds a like a banishment, and "fall asleep", which sounds precarious (and potentially painful).

Babies can become unsettled and resist sleep if our attitude towards bedtime is pitying, as in "poor baby has to go sleep"; when we're anticipating a battle: "uh-oh, this is going to be trouble"; or even when they sense our impatience: "you're tired, so hurry up and go to sleep already!" These attitudes make it far more difficult for our baby to do his or her job, which is to relax and let go enough to let sleep happen.

The most important thing to know about sleep is the most important thing to know about parenting in general: Babies are aware and competent whole people. They are listening, noticing, absorbing, primed to learn about us and life through our every interaction, no matter how subtle, whether we want them to or not.

With this truth in mind, here are a few other important – albeit subtle — things to know about babies and sleep:

Babies are easily over-stimulated and overtired. It's easy to underestimate the hyper-sensitivity of very young children, but remember – they haven't developed the filters we have.

Imagine your sensory volume switch cranked waaaay up all the time, and there's nothing you can do to turn it down or tune anything out. While this hyper-awareness is what makes babies phenomenal information gatherers, it also means they become overstimulated in environments we'd consider quite manageable. And overstimulation and overtiredness can mean crankiness, whining, crying, difficulties both falling asleep and staying asleep.

Being an aware baby is exhilarating, but also exhausting, and overtiredness can happen easily (As a mom, I seemed to miss this often myself). I often remind the parents in my classes how ultra-stimulating and tiring the ninety minutes we spend together each week are, even though our classes are relatively relaxed and quiet. The babies are absorbing the space, the energy of all the people, while also developing their motor, cognitive and social skills through self-chosen play. For them, it is exhausting!

Encouraging restorative shut-eye means keeping our eyes open to the threat of over-stimulation and fatigue and catching the sleep wave early. Some of the early signs of fatigue include slowing down, a lack of coordination and a slightly dazed appearance (which actually sound a lot like me at the end of the day).

Babies appreciate routine and develop habits readily. Our choices as parents define life for our babies; we teach them what to expect, and they will usually want to continue doing what they know (which makes sense, considering their new and often overwhelming world). So although sleep routines and preferences are individual to each family, they all have the tendency to become habit-forming.

One example that comes to mind: an infant I worked with who had become accustomed to sleeping while carried by her mum in a sling. The family ran into difficulties when they tried transitioning her to sleeping in a bed, because she had learned to sleep with her legs elevated, and also to fall asleep while nursing. When the parents tried to place her in a bed asleep, she would soon startle herself awake again as she felt her legs drop down onto the bed.

The parents eventually consulted a sleep expert who offered them a new plan. It included placing their baby in bed while she was still at least slightly awake, and turning her towards the bed initially so that she could see where she going before they placed her on her back. They then allowed her a few minutes to settle, which meant (as it often does) some stress-release crying.

I'm hoping no one reading will misinterpret this as a suggestion not to ever nurse infants to sleep or allow them to catnap in a carrier or in our arms. My advice is simply to keep in mind that our choices have an impact, because the conditions we create can become habits that can then become our baby's needs. While some babies will naturally transition out of these habits, others will find changes more difficult.

If changes in routines need to be made, communication and respect are imperative. As much as babies prefer the predictable and familiar, they are also capable of adapting to the changes we deem necessary, as long as our expectations are developmentally appropriate (in other words, we should not expect young infants to go all night without feeding, etc.).

I personally dislike the term 'sleep training', not only because it sounds unnatural and forced, but also because transitioning to healthier sleep habits is actually the opposite of training — it is more like *un* -training. We are respectfully un-training the children we've trained to be lulled to sleep by our rocking, bouncing, carrying and car rides. We are respectfully un-training the children we've conditioned to fall asleep (and, for some only, stay asleep) on the breast.

Our competent, aware babies can make these adjustments with a minimum of stress if we establish a respectful, trusting relationship by:

a) Developing a communicative relationship: The sooner we talk to our babies as if they can understand, the sooner we'll recognize that they *do* understand. For example, when we regularly ask our baby, "Are you ready for me to pick you up?" rather than swooping her up. And then we wait for her response and if a "yes" is indicated, we acknowledge, "Okay, I'm going to pick you up now." We begin to notice our baby tensing her body a bit in anticipation of being picked up. Eventually, she'll lift her arms towards ours.

b) Informing babies simply and honestly about changes we are making: "After your bath we'll nurse and then I'll sing a song while we snuggle and take you to your bed so you can rest. Usually we rock and rock, but tonight we'll snuggle and then say goodnight in your bed."

c) Supporting, accepting and acknowledging feelings: "You are upset. This feels very different, I know. You are used to rocking. I hear how upset you are. You are having a hard time relaxing, but you will soon."

Sleep requires letting go. Establishing healthy sleep rhythms for our cognizant babies means creating the conditions and adopting the practices that make it easier for them to let go of their fascinating world at bedtime. Our calm presence helps them to let go of stimulation, stress, excitement and other emotions they may have stored that day (or morning).

For our babies to let go, they need *us* to let go, which means bedtime is never a good time to express our worry, frustration, anger or engage in battles about sleep (ever tried to go to sleep wound-up or upset?).

Predictable bedtime routines that we repeat each day help babies learn to gradually let go and anticipate sleep, perhaps even look forward to it, as do soothing stories and lullabies.

"A nice bedtime habit to start with our child is to recapture the day. You can say, for example, "Today we went for a walk and it rained. We came home and had lunch, etc.' What we think is unimportant is important to a child – what she ate, where she was, and who she saw. Recapturing the day is a way of giving her security. She then carries the good feelings of the day into bed with her. You can also mention what will happen tomorrow. This connects the past, the present, and the future, and gives her life a connected flow..."
                    - Magda Gerber, *Your Self-Confident Baby*

Zzzzzzz...

7.

Sitting Babies Up: The Downside

Some might consider it social suicide to suggest negatives about a practice that probably 90 percent of parents do with their babies. Is it *really* worth the grief to get into it?

After struggling with this, my passion for natural gross motor development won out. So I sincerely hope that you'll read the following with an open mind (or stop now and skip to another chapter).

My husband and I sat our first baby up without a second thought, propping her on the couch at just a few weeks old to take pictures of her in her fabulous new baby wardrobe. When I look at those photos now, I realize this was not a flattering position. She looks slumped and frozen — neither comfy nor happy. In one particularly undignified shot she's dressed in a garish, orange court-jester-inspired jumpsuit and matching hat, a gift from a witty friend (with no kids). It's clear from the scowl on our newborn's face that she didn't see the humor.

By the time our baby was four months old, I was attending RIE classes and was encouraged to provide her abundant time to move freely and allow her to roll from back to tummy, pivot, scoot and eventually discover sitting all on her own.

I'll never forget the first time she managed to sit by herself. She had been rocking on her knees, then rolling back to her side and *almost* getting there for several days. Then, one morning, she was playing on the floor in a minuscule hotel room in Paris, and suddenly there she was, sitting in front of an armoire, surprised to find a reflection of herself in the mirror.

The splendor of "baby-owned" accomplishments like these is one of the reasons I recommend giving infants the opportunity to learn to sit on their own and not propping or positioning them. Here are some important others:

1. Natural Gross Motor Development: Many of the ideas Magda Gerber taught were based on the research and clinical work of renowned Hungarian pediatrician Emmi Pikler (1902-1984), who was Magda's friend and mentor. One of Dr. Pikler's revolutionary contributions to infant care developed from her keen interest in the physiology of motor development that was not restricted, aided or taught. Through her many years of research, observation and experience, Pikler concluded that when infant development is allowed to occur naturally and without interference, there are not only physical benefits such as grace and ease of movement, but psychological and cognitive benefits as well.

"The learning process will play a major role in the whole later life of the human being. Through this kind of development, the infant learns his ability to do something independently, through patient and persistent effort. While learning during motor development to turn on his belly, to roll, to creep, sit, stand, and walk, he is not only learning those

movements, but also 'how to learn'. He learns to do something on his own, to be interested, to try out, to experiment. He learns to overcome difficulties. He comes to know the joy and satisfaction that is derived from his success, the result of his patience and persistence."

    - Dr. Emmi Pikler, *Peaceful Babies – Contented Mothers*

2. Restricting movement: Sitting babies up prematurely prevents them from rolling, twisting, scooting, or doing much of anything else. When an infant is placed in this position before she is able to attain it independently, she usually cannot get out of it without falling, which does not encourage a sense of security or physical confidence.

The babies I've observed playing this way look as if they're pinned to the floor, immobile from the waist down. While other infants are moving their limbs freely on their backs, rolling from back to tummy and beginning to pivot, scoot or army crawl, the seated babies can only bend at the trunk to reach objects of interest. If a toy rolls out of reach, the seated babies must depend on an adult to get it back.

Of course, infants are brilliantly adaptive. I've seen babies routinely placed in this position learn to swivel around in a circle and eventually mobilize themselves by scooting on their bottoms.

3. Habits: Babies like to continue doing what they know (and the habits we create for them can easily become their "needs"). When we sit babies up, they usually begin to expect and want that. Conversely, if you don't sit a baby up, she won't desire the position.

If parents want to backtrack and try to break the sitting habit, there will probably be an adjustment period and some complaints from the baby, who has to be encouraged in small doses to get comfortable on her back. This is a position from which her motor development can progress naturally.

"Giving infants, even if they have developmental delays, the freedom to move in accordance with their innate impulses may seem radical, but it is essential to their becoming persons with uncompromised self esteem."
- Ruth Anne Hammond, *Respecting Babies*

4. Delaying, skipping motor milestones: When parents write to me concerned about their infants not reaching milestones like rolling or crawling, it often turns out that they've been restricting movement in devices like infant seats, jumpers and saucers, or sitting the baby up.

Babies can't be expected to develop motor skills without the time and freedom to do so. If they are stuck sitting, infants sometimes even skip the other important milestones (rolling, scooting and crawling).

"I believe in giving your baby a safe space in which to play and letting her move freely and develop on her own without assisting her. Refrain from propping her up to sit or helping her roll over. She has an innate desire to move through these developmental sequences and has inborn knowledge of how to do it in a way that is "right' for her. She does this at her own pace and she gets pleasure from doing it."
- Magda Gerber

5. Independent play: Sitting babies up is a major roadblock to independent play. Since premature sitting is a dependent, static position, babies aren't inclined to enjoy staying this way for very long (and this is assuming they don't fall over).

6. Flexibility, posture, form: Body scientist and Feldenkrais Practitioner Irene Lyon offers this perspective:

"Consider how hard it is for most adults to sit on the floor with their pelvis fully under them. More people are realizing how hard this is as sitting meditation becomes more en vogue, just as yoga made people realize how short their hamstrings are. But, if you give a kid the chance to find their own way to sitting, it means they have properly engineered their bodies in the best way possible for them through their own discovery and movement, and of course learning how to form curves in their spine and hips, how to find the flexibility in their ankle and knee joints. When given the chance to do it on their own, it is a gradual organic process and the form follows the functionality."

If you want to see a perfect example of a baby finding her own way, I strongly recommend watching Irene's 3-minute video "Baby Liv", which you can access on YouTube.

7. Loss of transitional postures: One example of a transitional posture is the 'reclining on one's side' position (which I fondly call "The Male Centerfold") that usually leads to sitting. There are many other postures as well that occur between the biggies like rolling, scooting and sitting. Some are variations unique to the particular child, and if we believe in the wisdom of the body (as I do), they each have a valuable developmental purpose. I remind parents to take pictures, because most of these are charming and short-lived.

8. What's the rush? Babies build self-confidence when they are trusted, accepted and appreciated for what they can (and choose to) do. They will achieve it all in their own time.

"I have asked parents, 'How old were you when you learned to sit?' So far, nobody could remember. What is the benefit of early sitting? Why are so many people hooked on concepts such as 'sooner is better'? Since our life span is getting longer, why not slow down? Why are concepts such as readiness and motivation hardly mentioned?"

– Magda Gerber

8.

How to Build Your Child's Focus and Attention Span

We don't think twice about interrupting infants and toddlers, mostly because we don't think to value what they are doing. At the same time, we want our children to be learners and achievers. We want them to be able to listen patiently in the classroom and have the tenacity to solve difficult problems and pursue their dreams. We want 'paying attention' to come naturally, learning skills to come joyfully and easily.

The first years of life are formative for developing focus and concentration. Here are several ways to foster a long attention span:

Minimal entertainment and stimulation. Babies are creatures of habit and can become accustomed to expect entertainment rather than doing what comes naturally — occupying themselves with their surroundings. Constant stimulation leads to an exhausted parent and an easily bored, over-stimulated child.

Infant expert Magda Gerber taught that babies don't naturally become bored. Parents do. Babies are entranced by the way their bodies can move and the sights, sounds, smells, nooks and crannies of life that we adults take for granted. They need uninterrupted time to experience those things and assimilate them.

No TV or videos for the first two years. TV and videos are the most drastic way to undermine your child's developing attention span because they engage and overwhelm his attention rather than encouraging him to actively flex his focus muscle.

Imagine the powerful pull of the TV screen in a restaurant. You can be sitting with the most fascinating people in the world, and still you find your eyes drawn to the damn TV. (For an in-depth study on the TV issue, I highly recommend *Endangered Minds: Why Children Don't Think – And What We Can Do About It* by Jane M. Healy, Ph.D.)

Create a safe, cozy "Yes" place. In order to remain occupied for extended periods of time, a baby must have a safe place. This can begin with a bassinet or crib, eventually a playpen, and finally a cordoned-off or gated play area. A too large area where there are unsafe objects available to a child is not the relaxed environment the baby needs for extensive concentration. Babies cannot play for long periods of time when they are distracted by the tension of parents worried about safety and the interruption of "No's".

Only simple, open-ended toys and objects. Unless distracted, babies are inclined to examine every inch of a simple object, like the pattern on a cloth napkin. They will experiment: wave it, mouth it, place it over their faces, and scrunch it into a ball. They are apt to tire of, or become over-stimulated by objects that they either cannot comprehend (like rattles and other mysterious noisemakers) or toys that they passively watch, listen to, and have a single function (like musical mobiles or wind-up toys). Those toys grab the child's attention rather than strengthening his ability to actively focus, investigate and interact, similar to the way TV and videos do.

Observe. And don't interrupt. Observing the way our babies choose to spend their time makes us realize that they are not just lying there, but actually *doing* something. That something might be gazing towards a window, at the ceiling fan, or grasping at dust particles in the sunlight.

Every time we interrupt our baby's musings we discourage his concentration. When we observe, we can see when there is a break in the action, i.e. the baby averts his gaze from the whiffle ball he was prodding with his fingers and turns to look at us. We can then ask to pick him up for a diaper change without diverting his attention and interfering with his train of thought.

Baby gets to choose. Simple fact: Children are more interested in the things they choose than the things we choose for them. Therefore, allowing a baby to choose what to do in his play environment rather than directing him to our choice of activity (a learning game, puzzle or flash card) will better engage his interest, focus and concentration.

Children who are given plenty of opportunities to focus for extended periods of time on activities they choose are better able to pay attention in situations later (like school) where activities are adult-prescribed.

Don't encourage distraction. It is common practice to distract a baby with a toy on the changing table to "get the job done." But this trains babies to *not* pay attention. Diaper changes, baths, and feedings are not dull, unpleasant chores for babies. Babies are interested in all aspects of their lives. They want to be included in each step of a task that involves them and be invited to participate as much as they are able.

When we teach a baby that he should NOT pay attention to activities he's an integral part of, how do we then expect him to develop a healthy attention span?

The ability to spend extended periods of time delving deeply, seeking greater understanding of an object or situation, can be developed and strengthened like a muscle. I don't pretend to be a PhD, but common sense and experience tells me that a home environment conducive to focus and attention can have a positive impact on – and maybe even prevent — some attention deficit disorders.

Focus is power. A long attention span is essential for creative, athletic and academic achievement. Attentive listeners make the best friends, spouses and parents.

So next time you check on your baby, tiptoe in and peek before saying "Hello."

9.

Infant Play – Great Minds at Work

I've observed hundreds of babies over twenty years and am comfortable that I have some insight into their worlds, but I still feel a little awkward when I describe 'infant play' to others. I sense the person thinking, "Oh yeah, right, infants *playing*."

But, actually, from the time a baby is weeks, even days old, she can begin the joyful habit of inner-directed play. And when we learn to recognize, appreciate and allow this invaluable element of an infant's life, amazing surprises are in store for us.

Play time for a young infant may look pretty boring to an untrained adult eye. We feel compelled to entertain a baby (as I did), or believe that she needs to be kept stimulated by continually moving with us through our daily affairs in a carrier or infant seat. Truthfully, babies don't need us to expend our energy occupying their time. In fact, keeping a baby busy undermines her natural desire to be an initiator of her own activities and absorb the world on her terms.

Babies are self-learners, and what they truly need (and pays enormous developmental benefits) is the time, freedom and trust to just "be".

We forget as adults that every mundane detail of the world is new and stimulating to an infant — every shape, contrast, and sound, even the slightest movement is fascinating. Life is a playground. So, infants are "playing" when they look around, listen, feel and smell the air, when they have the freedom to reach, grasp, twist their bodies, and think...think...think. (Wouldn't you just love to know what babies are thinking?)

I first noticed one of my babies playing on the changing table when he was nine days old. As we were finishing his diaper change I saw him gazing at a shadow on the wall, completely absorbed. I took a deep breath, stopped myself from interrupting...and just waited. When he finally looked up at me two or three minutes later, I asked, "Do you want me to pick you up?" And when his eyes seemed to say "Yes," I did.

Respecting these important personal moments when our infant is engaged in thought - *not interrupting* -- encourages longer periods of play that can extend to hours as a baby grows, through toddlerhood and beyond.

Babies tend to be more deeply engaged when they are trusted with their own play agendas rather than responding to ours. When babies are "writer, director and lead actor" of their playtime, as Magda Gerber recommended, they develop strong cognitive learning skills and nurture their natural abilities to explore, imagine, and create.

Our role is to design a safe space with a few simple toys and objects. The sensory delight of the outdoors is always preferable when possible. We make sure the baby can move freely, first by lying on her back. Then we let go of all expectations (an interesting challenge) and allow our baby to do what she wishes.

Simple objects that a child can use creatively in multiple ways are best, like balls of all sizes, cotton napkins, large plastic chains or rings, stacking cups, simple baby dolls, etc. As the infant becomes a toddler, puzzles, board books, climbing structures, more complex equipment can be added, always keeping in mind that we want to encourage active learning, child-directed problem solving, and creative experimentation rather than "doing it right".

For a video example of an infant blissfully at play and the same child at 2-years-old, you can watch: *Smart Baby's Self-Directed Play (RIE Baby)* on YouTube.

10.

Doctors, Dentists, Haircuts

I have had many surprises since becoming a mom. I found out that children under the age of six never walk down a hallway when they can run; that corn kernels pass through the body whole; and that boys have a testosterone-powered impulse to test the breaking point of everything, especially new toys, with predictable results.

But the biggest surprise of all was the discovery that babies and toddlers can actually enjoy, and even look forward to getting a haircut, or visiting the doctor or dentist. (Certainly, not the way I ever felt!) And all I had to do to make this possible was to help my baby 'look forward' to these routine events by honestly preparing her for the situations beforehand.

When I began attending RIE parenting classes as a new mom, I adopted the habit of telling my baby what was happening to her, and especially what was *about* to happen. I told her that I was going to pick her up, place her on a changing table, or do anything that involved her before I did it.

I learned that babies crave predictability. They like the teensy bit of control they feel when they can anticipate what will happen next. It makes their world feel a little less overwhelming and more secure to know, for example, that after bath time they will put on pajamas, hear a lovely song, and then be carried over to help draw the shades before being placed in their bed. Babies like to be included in a process, to participate as much as possible, even if it just means being informed about all that is happening to them.

When babies are treated with this kind of respect, they are surprisingly cooperative, because they are aware and engaged. But when we scoop a baby up without a word, or distract her with a toy to get a diaper changed quickly, we discourage her involvement and make her feel manipulated into compliance rather than like a partner in an intimate activity.

Even though babies cannot speak, they are whole people, capable of participating actively in a relationship with us, and in their lives. The sooner we honestly take them in and invite them to join us, the sooner they will.

When my baby was around twelve months old, I prepared her for the doctor's office in advance. I talked to her at home on the morning of our appointment, told her where we were going and what would happen there. I told her about the scale, the stethoscope, about the doctor looking into her eyes with a light, feeling her belly and looking into her mouth. And if I had thought she was getting a shot that day, I would have told her about that too, and right before she was injected I'd warn, "This may hurt or sting."

When my daughter and I arrived at the doctor's office she had been hearing all about, I could sense her eager anticipation, and when the doctor finally came into the examining room, she was quiet, attentive, breathlessly waiting for all my predictions to be fulfilled.

Unfortunately, this well-meaning doctor launched into a comedy/magic routine, whizzing that little pen light all over like a firefly in his attempt to distract, telling her, "I see a birdie in your ear!", and then sneaking in the peeks he needed for his examination.

My baby was nonplussed. I moderated. I told her what the doctor was actually doing so that she could stay involved and at least mentally participate as much as possible. He is a fine physician but has a common view about children — that they cannot be trusted with the truth and need to be tricked and entertained to distraction for him to get his job done.

Happily, my daughter enjoyed her first doctor's office experience enough to want to go back. She reacted with similar interest to wearing a giant bib at the barbershop and feeling the snip-snip of scissors cutting her hair, and she always looked forward to the dentist, even though she had to keep her mouth open for a long, long time.

No question my children appreciate a lollipop, a new toothbrush, or an "I Have Great Teeth" sticker. But I came to the conclusion a long time ago that the honest preparation that led to their active involvement in those early experiences with the doctor, dentist and hairstylist is the reason my children still like going.

Or maybe they're just weird kids.

11.

Calming Your Clingy Child

It's good to feel needed, but when we become parents, we realize we never *really* knew "needy". As Magda Gerber aptly noted, parenting brings with it a "feeling of un-freeness", whether we're in the presence of our children or not.

Toward the end of the first year of life (when children become more aware of the separation between themselves and their parents), and periodically throughout the early years, we primary caregivers often become the sole object of our child's desire.

Clingy periods tend to coincide with children taking developmental steps toward independence (like learning to walk). Sometimes they occur when children face new situations or transitions (for example, mom's expecting). As understandable as this is, it's still intensely stifling, frustrating and guilt-inducing when our lovable ball-and-chain can't let us out of her sight for even a second.

When babies are around 9-12 months old, parents in my classes often share a common, enlightening scenario: "All I'm doing is making a quick trip to the bathroom or taking a shower, and my baby screams and cries inconsolably. What should I do?!" Obviously, they're deeply distressed about putting their baby through such agony — but then it turns out the baby wasn't alone after all. She was with her doting dad. Hmm...

Not to downplay infant emotions, but is this baby in desperate need? Or is this a healthy expression of her developing will? Either way, the situation is tough for baby, mom and dad.

Here's what I suggest to ease the anxiety all around and help everyone cope when children are feeling clingy:

Encourage autonomy. The way we perceive our children has a profound influence on them. While some experts refer to newborns as "helpless", Magda Gerber made the seemingly minor — but important — distinction that babies are *dependent*, not helpless. She believed that babies are innately capable if we allow them to be, and this has been affirmed for me a thousand times over. Magda called this having "basic trust" in babies, and it is key to her approach.

One of the things most babies can do (and seem to greatly enjoy doing) is spend baby-directed time on their own. We might first notice this when we see our newborn awaken and look around for a while before indicating she needs us. Delicate seeds of independence are sown when we refrain from showering our babies with love at these times and just quietly observe. If we provide scattered minutes like these in a safe place, they can then evolve into longer and longer periods of baby me-time — a time for exploring, learning, creating, communing with "self". Granting children this uninterrupted time and space from the beginning, but never forcing it, fosters healthy autonomy.

This bit of independence doesn't eliminate separation anxiety and clinginess, but it definitely seems to lessen the frequency, intensity and duration of the episodes. And that makes sense, because children who have tasted autonomy have the inexorable knowledge that they can be more than fine for a time on their own.

Don't overreact. Babies are aware and impressionable, which means that they are constantly receiving messages from us through our responses and behavior. For example, if our baby is trying to roll over and we instantly swoop in and turn her over or scoop her up at the first sound of struggle, she's going to believe she's incapable of coping with even the smallest struggles herself.

On the other hand, if we sit down next to our baby, bend down to her level, acknowledge her feelings and efforts, wait a little and then — if she continues crying — ask her if she wants to cuddle in our lap, she will receive an equally loving, far more empowering message. Often she'll end up choosing to persevere with her task once she's been heard and understood.

These messages we transmit to our children add up to them feeling either secure and competent, or dependent on our magic powers to rescue them.

Separate with confidence. Again, children are very sensitive to our feelings. If we are feeling ambivalent, upset, guilty, etc. about leaving them in a safe place while we separate, there's little chance that our child is going to be able to let us go gracefully. If we're unsure, how can our child possibly feel secure?

So I recommend **always** telling your child you will go (sneaking out creates much more anxiety and mistrust), and doing so with kindness, assuredness and confidence in your child as fully capable of handling this situation. "I'm going to the bathroom and will be back in

5 minutes." If you can remember to, it's always best to leave out the "okay?" at the end, since that implies uncertainty or a need for the child's permission. If the child cries as you are trying to leave, acknowledge, "I hear you. You don't want me to go, but I'll be back."

Don't talk children out of their feelings. Acknowledge your child's feelings about your separation without even a hint of judgments like, "But I've played with you all morning!" Fully accept them. Encourage the parent or caregiver who remains with the child to support the child to grieve your temporary loss for as long as they need to while calmly assuring the child, "Mommy will come back." Ask them not to distract, "shush" or tell the child "you're okay", just keep acknowledging the feelings, listening, offering support and hugs if the child wishes. Children's feelings are valid and need to be treated as such.

Give children confidence-building opportunities to separate (and return to their secure base). Here's a reminder I give parents in my classes, especially when they are concerned about their child clinging and not playing: We are almost always the ones who initiate separations with our children. Children also need to feel trusted to separate and return as needed. (Confidence in our children to experience this is essential to them forming secure attachments according to John Bowlby's Attachment Theory.)

But child-led separation can't happen if we follow babies and toddlers around. This is one of the reasons in RIE Parent/Infant Guidance Classes we recommend parents find a seat and stay put. When we follow children in safe play situations like these, we send them the message that we don't believe them capable of being away from us. Perhaps we do this because we think we have to show our child how to play (don't worry, we don't). Or could it be that we're the ones having trouble separating here?

Staying in one place is especially important in group situations, because then the child knows exactly where we are, which frees her to separate with confidence when she's ready.

Accept clinginess readily. I advise never resisting clinginess. Yes, there are times we need (or want) to separate, and that's a healthy and positive thing to do. Parents' needs and limits are an integral part of the parent/child relationship. Taking care of ourselves (even when our child disagrees) and feeling confident about that is vital to our bond.

Then there are those times at the playgroup, the park, a party, or even just at home when we might *expect* our child to be out playing or socializing, but our child is glued to us. Release those expectations or wishes — let clinginess be. In fact, welcome it. Don't entertain; just let the child sit with you and watch. Coaxing, redirecting, pointing out all the wonderful children and toys our child could be playing with only intensifies her desire to cling.

When we trust that our child needs to be close and give her the assurance that we don't resist this in the least, separation anxiety eases.

So whenever possible — give in wholeheartedly. Hold your child close and try to imagine the day she no longer wants to spend time on your lap (or doesn't fit very well). Ugh, never mind, let's not go there.

12.

A Magic Word for Parenting
(And 10 Ways to Use It)

Madga Gerber extolled the power of a single word that is fundamental to her child care philosophy. This word reflects a core belief in a baby's natural abilities, respects his unique developmental timetable, fulfills his need to experience mastery, be a creative problem solver, and to express feelings (even those that are hard for us to witness).

The word is a simple, practical tool for understanding babies, providing love, attention and trust for humans of all ages. The word is WAIT. Here's how it works:

Wait for the development of an infant or toddler's motor skills, toilet learning, language and other preschool learning skills. Notice a child's satisfaction, comfort and pride when he is able to show you what he is ready to do, rather than the other way around. As Magda often said, "Readiness is when they do it." Ready babies do it better (Hmm... a bumper sticker?), and they own their achievements completely, building self-confidence that lasts a lifetime.

Wait before interrupting. Give babies the opportunity to continue what they are doing, learn more about what interests them, develop longer attention spans and become independent self-learners.

When we wait while a newborn gazes at the ceiling and allow him to continue his train of thought, he is encouraged not only to keep thinking, but to keep trusting his instincts. Refrain from interrupting whenever possible. It gives your child the message that you value his chosen activities (and therefore him).

Wait for problem solving and allow a child the resilience-building struggle and frustration that usually precedes accomplishment. Wait to see first what a child is capable of doing on his own.

When a baby is struggling to roll from back to tummy, try comforting with gentle words of encouragement before intervening and interrupting his process. Then if frustration mounts, pick him up and give him a break rather than turning him over and 'fixing' him. This encourages our baby to try, try again and eventually succeed, rather than believe himself incapable and expect others to do it for him. This holds true for the development of motor skills, struggles with toys, puzzles and equipment, even self-soothing abilities like finding his thumb rather than giving him a pacifier.

Wait for discovery rather than showing a child her new toy and how it works.

"When you teach a child something, you take away forever his chance of discovering it for himself."

–Jean Piaget

Wait and observe to see what the child is really doing before jumping to conclusions. A baby reaching towards a toy might be satisfied to be stretching his arm and fingers, not expecting to accomplish a task. A toddler looking through a sliding glass door might be practicing standing or enjoying the view and not necessarily eager to go outside.

Wait for conflict resolution and give babies the opportunity to solve problems with their peers, which they usually do quite readily if we can remain calm and patient. And what may look like conflict to an adult is often just "playing together" through an infant or toddler's eyes.

Wait for readiness before introducing new activities so children can be active participants, embrace experiences more eagerly and confidently, comprehend and learn far more.

It's hard to wait to share our own exciting childhood experiences (like shows, theme parks or dance classes) with our children, but sooner is almost never better, and our patience always pays off.

Wait for a better understanding of what babies need when they cry. When we follow the impulse most of us have to quell our children's tears as quickly as possible, we can end up projecting and assuming needs rather than truly understanding what our child is communicating.

Wait for feelings to be expressed so that our children can fully process them. Our child's cries can stir up our own deeply suppressed emotions; make us impatient, annoyed, uneasy, and even angry or fearful. But children need our non-judgmental acceptance of their feelings and our encouragement to allow them to run their course.

Wait for ideas from children before offering suggestions of your own. This encourages them to be patient thinkers and brain-stormers. Countless times I've experienced the miracle of waiting before giving my brilliant two cents while children play, or providing play ideas when children seem bored. Biting my tongue for a few minutes, maybe saying some encouraging words to a toddler like, "It's hard to know what to do sometimes, but you are creative, I know you'll think of something" is usually all that it takes for the child to come up with an idea. And it's bound to be more imaginative, interesting and appropriate than anything I could have thought of.

Best of all, the child receives spectacular affirmations:

1) I am a creative thinker and problem solver;

2) I can bear discomfort, struggle and frustration;

3) Boredom is just the time and space between ideas (and sometimes the wellspring of genius.)

Instincts may tell us that waiting is *un*-caring, *un*-helpful and confidence-shaking — until the results are proven to us. Sitting back patiently and observing often feels counterintuitive, so even if we know and appreciate the magic that can happen when we wait, it usually involves a conscious effort. But it's worth it.

13.

Allowing Your Toddler to Succeed

My parent/toddler classroom is set up with simple toys, platforms, climbing structures, common household objects. One morning I included a large, white plastic jar with a wide screw-on lid. I put several plastic chain links inside the jar and, as I later realized, closed it a bit too tightly.

The parents and toddlers started to arrive and I welcomed Jenna, a twenty-month-old girl, accompanied for the first time by her Aunt Lisa. After introductions, the parents settled in and the children began to play.

Jenna began bringing objects to her aunt, a common practice of toddlers. Jenna gave Lisa a stuffed dog and Lisa turned it around on her lap to face Jenna. Then Jenna handed Lisa some rings that were hooked together. Lisa took the rings apart for her. Jenna carried over a toy bus and Lisa rolled it on the ground. The pattern of Jenna hauling toys to Lisa continued, and Lisa, wanting to share in the play and show congeniality, responded to each gift of a toy with her own new action.

By playing for Jenna, even in this subtle and well-meaning manner, Lisa was making Jenna the audience rather than the actor.

It is difficult for adults to see how easily their actions can dominate when they play with a child. When an adult does more than just respond to what a child is doing, the interaction expresses the adult's interests rather than the child's. While other toddlers were exploring, Jenna was watching her aunt.

I hoped Jenna's attention would shift during our time of quiet observation. I reminded the parents that we would, for ten or fifteen minutes, attempt to empty our minds of expectations and projections and simply observe the children with as much objectivity as possible. I added that we should interact with a child if they looked to us to do so, but we should keep our responses minimal so as not to engage the children too much.

When caregivers practice this kind of observation, they gain valuable insights into the minds of children. Watching a child who is engrossed in exploring his surroundings, interacting with his peers and experimenting with activities he designs can be illuminating, even astonishing. If a picture is worth a thousand words, then a live demonstration is worth a million in the way that it helps us to understand our child and his needs.

When Lisa stopped playing with Jenna and just graciously accepted the objects Jenna presented to her, Jenna began to demonstrate inner-directed exploration. She brought the bus over to a large box filled with balls of all sizes and tested its ability to drive over the bumps inside the box for several minutes. Eventually she moved on to another toy.

While I was watching a second child, Jenna apparently discovered the jar I had placed in one of the large wooden cubes. I saw Jenna bring the jar, rattling with the links inside it, to Lisa. Holding the large jar with both hands, Jenna extended it towards her aunt, and I feared the worst. Surely, kind-hearted Lisa would not be able to resist opening the jar for her. "Please don't open that for her," I implored. "Trust me."

The next thing that happened nearly made me erupt in laughter. In response to my admonition to Lisa not to open the jar, Jenna turned and gave me a long stare as if in indignant outrage, but it was likely just surprise. She finally looked back at the jar, now in her aunt's hands, but made no attempt to open it herself. Jenna did not appear to be frustrated. She has two older brothers and may have been accustomed to having others solve problems for her. This was all the more reason why I hoped Jenna would be encouraged to take more initiative.

But Jenna's opportunity to experiment with the jar ended when Emily, a girl who had joined the class recently, walked over to Jenna and seized the jar. Emily carried the jar to her dad, who was in class for his second time; she appeared confident that he would save the day.

Before he could act, I said, "You're asking your dad to open that. I don't think he can." Emily's dad, Jim, looked at me with an uneasy smirk. I shook my head slightly and smiled weakly. I wished I could have made a more honest statement to Emily about her dad's jar opening abilities, but in my single-minded desire to make Jim resist her request, a little white lie had spilled out. Jim held the jar but did not open it, although I could tell how badly he wanted to do so.

At this point, I had asked two adults to go against their instincts when they wanted to help a child, and I found myself in a precarious situation. If this experiment did not have a happy ending, I'd have an entire omelette on my face. But I took solace in noticing that Emily, like Jenna, was not the least bit upset. She seemed perplexed by the strange way the adults were acting, but not discouraged at all. She made an attempt to unscrew the jar while her father held it for her. Then she brought the jar over to me.

Emily's gesture eased my mind, because while I still felt like the villain in the room, I remembered Magda Gerber saying that when a toddler hands you something it is an indication that the child trusts you. "You're asking me to hold the jar?" I inquired.

As I held the jar Emily made another attempt to turn the lid. "You're trying to open the top. It's hard to open." I then *discreetly* touched the side of the lid that faced me with my thumb, loosening it the teeniest bit. When Emily tried again she was able to slowly unscrew the lid and open the jar. She flashed me a look and I said with a smile, "You opened it." A few moments later Emily put the lid back on and then opened it on her own again.

Children need the opportunity to solve problems on their own. Parents can create (rather than deprive children of) this opportunity by resisting an automatic impulse to 'open the jar'.

Yes, it is counter-intuitive to refrain from assisting a child! But when we help a child to do something she might be able to do for herself, we are robbing her of a vital learning experience and ultimately not helping at all.

Children see adults as magical and all-powerful. When we intervene in a child's every struggle and fix every problem, we reinforce this view. But if parents and caregivers can believe in a child's capabilities, and if they can let a child work to figure things out and even allow for frustration and "failure", then the child will show us that she is indeed capable of more than we can imagine.

14.

The Therapeutic Power of Play

The most illuminating example of therapeutic play I've heard was a story shared by Magda Gerber. She had been asked to visit a child care center, and while touring the infant playroom with the center's director she noticed one of the children holding a spoon and placing the tip at the opening of a baby doll's bottom.

The director also noticed, and she corrected the boy, "No, that goes in the mouth." She demonstrated for him, taking the spoon away and holding it up to the baby doll's mouth. As she returned to her discussion with Magda, the boy reverted to his previous action. Again, the director stopped and corrected him.

It was late in the day, and the parents were beginning to arrive. The boy's mother was one of the first. She picked up her boy and, as she was leaving, stopped to say to the director, "I forgot to tell you this morning that poor Johnny had to have an enema at the doctor's yesterday. He didn't like it *at all*."

Zillions of studies prove the awesome benefits of play, and as Magda's experience illustrates, one of the most profound is its use as a natural and powerful self-therapy tool. Children use play instinctively to process both environmental stress and inner-conflict. Play therapy helps them to make sense of confusing and bothersome events they might have been exposed to, eases worry and fear. It is especially valuable in the early years before children can verbalize their feelings. Children "play out" disturbing feelings when they can't tell us what's wrong or ask us "What's that?" or "Why?" To encourage play therapy:

1. Let go of judgment, expectations and play agendas. Let play belong to your child. Rather than interfere (as the director in Magda's example did), allow your child to be playwright, director and lead actor when he plays. Relegate yourself to set design by creating a safe, enriching environment with open-ended, simple toys and objects where your baby can explore and experiment. Then let him mess it up and redesign as he wishes. Never interrupt unnecessarily.

2. Take it outdoors whenever possible. Create a safe, enclosed outdoor play space with a chair and table nearby where you can relax (and maybe even do a little work) while your baby enjoys the therapeutic benefits of fresh air and nature. When the weather cooperates, move your life outdoors. Your children will sleep better, play better and even eat better. As a friend of mine once noted, "Food tastes better outside."

3. Nurture the self-directed play habit. Play is a natural inclination for babies and they love it, but it's up to us to begin the habit – to make it an essential part of their day. Young infants can (and will) let us know when they need to be held, but it is nearly impossible for a months-old baby to indicate "I'd like a little time to move freely and do what I want". And *doing what I want* is the key to play therapy.

Begin by placing an infant on her back and observing her response. If the baby complains tell her you hear her, ask her what she needs and if she wants to be picked up. Don't jump the gun. Sometimes, like all of us, a baby just wants us to listen and try to understand.

Brief episodes of this kind of "play" in which your baby might look around, stretch and twist, experiment with the workings of her limbs, and study her fascinating hands will extend into longer periods. Your baby's self-directed play soon becomes the highlight of your day together.

4. Watch, learn and appreciate. Most therapeutic play is far less obvious than the example of the boy and the spoon, especially before children are able to talk. Usually it's below the radar and undetectable to us. We're left wondering what our babies might be processing, if anything. And that will remain a mystery.

But since birth itself is stressful, even the youngest infants could conceivably have issues to work through. Honing our observation skills helps us detect the more subtle examples.

In a recent class, a 16-month-old toddler did something I've never seen before. She had recently become a big sister and was separated from her mother for several days due to complications during the birth. We have a row of three large wooden boxes in the RIE playroom. One of them has a small round hole cut out at the top. This little girl took the largest baby doll and managed to shove it down through the hole -- which wasn't easy. Yet she did it again, and again, and again.

Hmmm...

15.

7 Myths That Discourage Independent Play

The value of child-directed play is universally recognized and one of the few aspects of child-rearing that experts and thought leaders agree on. Independent play makes for highly productive, happily occupied kids, which in turn makes for happier, calmer parents. And it's natural — the desire and ability to create play is inborn. So, what could possibly go wrong?

Parents often share with me the difficulties they're having establishing the independent play habit for their kids. They tell me their infants cry when they're placed down, their toddlers won't play unless parents play with them, or their preschoolers need constant entertainment and direction.

Most of these problems stem from common misconceptions about independent play (all of which I once had):

Play Myth #1: Babies can't do it.

"Infancy is a time of great dependence. Nevertheless babies should be allowed to do things for themselves from the very beginning."

– Magda Gerber

Perhaps the most striking difference between Magda Gerber's Educaring Approach and other child-rearing methodologies is her disagreement with the common perception of infants as helpless. Infants are certainly dependent, she believed, but not helpless. She and her mentor Dr. Emmi Pikler perceived even the youngest infants as capable self-learners, able to initiate play and exploratory activities, experience mastery, engage directly with their environment and participate in communicative mind-to-mind partnerships with caregivers.

Brain studies conducted by psychologists like Alison Gopnik, Elizabeth Spelke and Paul Bloom confirmed Gerber and Pikler's views (finally). Infant minds are now proven to be up and running.

But this capable, competent infant is at odds with the more passive, helpless infant conceived by Dr. William Sears, influential writer Jean Leidloff and others. In their popular model based on ancestral practices, babies are dependent on their caregivers for entertainment and education and need almost constant physical contact to feel connected. The focus of this approach is carrying the baby for the majority of the day.

Establishing the habit of free play requires a quite different perception and focus — creating a safe play space and trusting the baby to initiate worthwhile independent activities. Of course, infants need lots of attentive holding and cuddling, but in Gerber's model, they also need play. She noted that infants can clearly indicate when they need to be held, but they can't enjoy playing independently until *we believe* they have something to do.

Play Myth #2: If a baby cries when she's placed down, she must not like playing. The best way for babies to begin free play is on their backs, because this is the position in which they have the most freedom, autonomy and mobility (try your tummy and then your back to see for yourself).

When parents tell me their baby cries as soon as she is placed down on her back, it is usually for one of these reasons:

a) The baby is placed down abruptly or without a word. Capable (dependent, rather than helpless) babies are whole people, and they need to be our communication partners. They need to be listened to and also spoken to respectfully about what will happen to them. "Now I will put you down on the blanket to play." Then let's say the baby cries. "Oh, you weren't ready?" The parent might then lie down next to the baby and caress her. "Was that too fast for you? I'm right here for you."

If the crying continues, the baby needs to be picked up but can remain in the parent's lap until she feels settled and comfortable enough in her surroundings to try playing again.

b) The baby is used to being carried, propped or positioned. Young children are adaptive but usually prefer to do what they are used to doing. In this brand new world, babies understandably crave the familiar, and they develop habits quickly. Habits like being carried or seated in an upright position often seem to become the child's "needs", even though these needs were actually created by the parents' choices.

Developing the free play habit is also a choice. It works best when parents prioritize it by making uninterrupted play the focus of the baby's "spare time" between naps and attentive feedings and diaper changes.

If parents want to make a transition from carrying or propping babies into independent play, the key is to introduce the new experience gradually and responsively with honest communication ("This is different, isn't it?") and patience.

c) The parent places the baby down and immediately leaves. No one likes to feel dumped. Parents usually need to begin play by holding the baby while seated on the floor and then stay there for a while after the baby's placed down. If the parent decides to leave, the baby must be told, or trust in the parent (and in play) can be undermined.

Play Myth #3: Play means "doing" something. Often the richest, most productive play doesn't look like much because it's dawdling, imagining, daydreaming, big picture thinking. To encourage this kind of play we must: first, value it; second, observe it; and lastly, not interrupt. The secret to not interrupting is to refrain from speaking to children until they initiate eye contact.

(Side note: Happily occupied babies don't feel neglected because adults aren't engaging them -- even if several minutes have passed. They know quite well how to ask for attention. Trust your baby.)

Play Myth #4: Gated play areas are restrictive jails. A safe space is essential for fostering independent play. Free roaming babies that follow parents around, even in the most baby-proofed home, don't focus on play as well or feel as truly free as babies in secure areas. Independent play requires a place free of "no's" and a relaxed, trusting parent who mostly stays put in order to be the secure base young explorers need.

Play Myth #5: Independent play means leaving children alone. One of the many positives about independent play is that once it's established in a safe space parents can usually leave their content, occupied child alone briefly while they do chores, use the bathroom, check email etc.

But the most valuable child-directed play is fostered when we learn a new way to enjoy playing *with* our kids, one that is mostly about observing and responding, less about actively participating. It's natural to want to interact, but parent participation has a tendency to take over. The more we are playing, the more our child is following our lead rather than creating and initiating plans of his or her own.

Parents often ask me what they can do to wean older children off the play dependencies they've unwittingly created. Generally, the process is to first believe our child capable and accept "not having anything to do" (and our child's frustration about that) as perfectly okay. Then relax, stay put and let the child decide to explore and return to you.

Play Myth #6: When children get frustrated or ask for help, we should solve the problem for them. As tempting as it is to fix situations for our children when it takes us all of two seconds, we are far more encouraging when we allow frustration, give verbal support, let go of results (since children often don't care about them as much as we do), and perhaps help in a very small way, so that the child is doing much more than we are.

When children ask for help, reflect and then ask questions: "So, you want to draw a dog? What kind of ears do you want the dog to have? Oh, the kind that point up? Show me what you mean." You might even resort to allowing the child to move your hand while you hold the pencil, but do all you can to give ownership of play to your child, which also means allowing some activities to be left unfinished.

Play Myth #7: It's our job to entertain and play with our children. There's definitely some truth to this one. Bonding through fun with our children is one of our jobs, but if we've encouraged kids to love playing independently, playtime together seldom feels like a chore, especially once we've discovered the joy of taking a back seat and trusting our child to drive.

As my own kids have gotten older, an invitation to play with them is such a rare and precious treat that I'll gladly drop everything. Come to think of it, I'm often the one asking!

16.

Nourishing Our Baby's Healthy Eating Habits

If we are what we eat, then aren't we also a product of the *way* we eat?

As busy new parents, we're usually first focused on the mechanics of breast or bottle-feeding, then the intricacies of introducing solids: when to start, which foods, in what order, how much, and how to provide the best nutrition.

But most of us also hope to foster healthy eating behaviors in our children. We want to do all in our power to prevent eating disorders, childhood obesity, vitamin deficiencies, and even the subtler issues we parents struggle with like the impulse to clean our plates or eat for emotional reasons.

Humans are creatures of habit, and the first years in a child's life are by far the easiest time to establish healthy ones. Here are some feeding suggestions advised by infant specialist Magda Gerber that help establish positive eating behaviors:

Relax, enjoy breast or bottle feedings. Make eating a focused, intimate, stress-free time together. Prepare the way for family dinners by making feedings a time for intimacy and social exchange. When we turn off the phone, computer, TV, and avoid other distractions to make feeding time sacred, we benefit our babies in several ways:

a) Babies are refueled by the loving attention they get while nursing or bottle-feeding to then enjoy time playing independently.

b) They learn that eating is a time to be mentally present rather than being taught to ignore the experience by a distracted parent.

c) Most importantly, our baby feels respected and valued when she is asked to actively participate in a feeding experience with us rather than just being fed.

I recently spoke with a mother who didn't believe she should pay attention to her son while he breastfed because whenever she talked to him he stopped nursing. I thought *what a polite boy to stop sucking to listen to what his mom was saying!* It sounded to me like he was trying his best to engage.

Tune in and take care to not overfeed. Paying attention to our baby during feedings also helps develop her internal cues to signal fullness. A recent study reported in *Science Daily* concluded that "tuning in" comes more easily when we breastfeed because, according to researcher Katherine F. Isselmann, M.P.H., "...with breast-feeding, the ability to measure in ounces how much a baby has eaten isn't there, so mothers can become more in tune with when their babies are done eating and babies are able to develop their own internal cues to signal when they feel full."

The same study compared preschool-aged children who had been breastfed with those who had been bottle fed with pumped breast milk and found that breastfed children could more easily determine when they were full. They also had a lower body mass index (BMI) than those fed by bottle.

If we bottle-feed, we must make a concerted effort to tune in to our baby's signals and be less focused on the ounces in the bottle.

Be careful with comfort food. Nursing a baby when she cries for reasons other than hunger, or rewarding or soothing children with food can create dependencies — a slippery slope. Ideally, these are exceptions, not the rule.

We are always teaching our children, and the safest lesson for our babies to learn about food is to drink when thirsty, eat when hungry.

Small portions and no "one more bites". When introducing solids, Magda Gerber suggested placing a very small amount of food in the baby's dish (with a larger bowl nearby), so that rather than feeling overwhelmed by too much food, the baby has the opportunity to signal for more.

We want to trust our babies to be in charge of their appetites, to indicate a desire for food by opening their mouths when we present them with a bite or spoonful. "Here comes the airplane" or "Just one more bite" coaxing can turn feeding into something our babies do to please us. It can encourage overeating, or make eating a power struggle.

To give babies even more opportunity for active participation when they eat, offer an extra spoon so she can practice. But when practicing becomes "playing with food", gently discourage it.

Highchair-free eating. Highchairs are considered a baby care staple, but Magda taught a unique approach to feeding babies without them. Magda's method is conducive to intimacy during feedings and also encourages our baby's independence.

Briefly: If solids are introduced before a baby is able to sit well and autonomously – meaning not propped or positioned, but able to attain a sitting position easily, entirely on their own – the baby is fed while reclining in the parent's arms on the parent's lap at the table.

Then, when the baby sits easily and independently, you can transition to a small table (like a breakfast-in-bed tray with legs, a wooden footstool with a level top, one of the wonderful kidney-shaped tables we use in RIE parenting classes, or something you or your talented carpenter husband can make). The baby sits on the floor, then later on a small stool or chair, while you sit across the table from her.

Toddlers love the independence they have when they can sit with their feet on the floor. They also appreciate the freedom to leave the table to signal they are finished eating rather than waiting to be removed from a highchair.

(Please check out the YouTube video that demonstrates: *Babies With Table Manners at RIE).*

No squat-and-gobble. Sit while eating, wherever and whenever. Sitting down while eating, even if it's just for snacks on a patch of grass in the park, helps prevent choking accidents and encourages relaxed, attentive eating. It's also good manners, especially when visiting the homes of others (who might not welcome a trail of cracker crumbs).

Asking a baby to sit when he eats is a sensible first behavior boundary. Don't let your toddler trick you into following him around with food in your hand. When infants and toddlers are hungry, they are absolutely capable of sitting down if we are consistent and clear about expecting it.

Eating while playing, playing while eating. Help your child learn to keep activities separate to help delineate meals and snacks as times to focus on food. Asking a child to sit (rather than climb monkey bars) while he eats is one way; keeping toys away from the table is another. Ask your toddler to please put his toy down until he is finished eating.

Don't worry. Babies, especially when they become toddlers, don't always eat the way we expect them to, and it's easy to become anxious if our child doesn't seem to be eating enough, especially if he isn't gaining weight normally. Of course we must check in regularly with our baby's doctor, explore possible allergies, illnesses or digestive issues. But try to be calm during baby's mealtimes. He senses our tension, and it can make eating more difficult for him in the short term, and possibly contribute to problems down the road.

Model healthy eating. We know we should walk the walk, but darn, we *like* to eat while we're standing up and running around. This is yet another instance when our babies make us better.

Only our baby can know his own appetite. So our goal might be to encourage him to stay attuned, to keep listening and trusting his tummy. And if he establishes healthy eating behaviors in these formative first years...we can all fudge later.

17.

Best Ways to Encourage Toddlers to Talk

First, let's clarify something that will hopefully bring relief: Encouraging our children to talk is *not* about chattering incessantly in order to expose them to as many words as possible (30,000 by age three is the magic number, according to some experts).

If you hear this advice, don't listen, because your babies won't either.

Honestly, can you think of anything more off-putting than someone blabbering for the sake of blabbering? Even our adoring babies, the captive audiences they are, will tune out (because they're unable to ask you to stop).

On the other hand, it's true that encouraging language development is about the quality and quantity of the words we speak. The great news is that both come naturally when we perceive babies as whole people — able communicators ready to be informed about the happenings in their lives, and in turn share their thoughts and feelings.

Comprehend this simple truth, interact naturally, and we've got the language lessons nailed. Here are some specifics:

1. Two-way communication from the beginning. From the time our babies are born, they need to know that we not only tell them what's happening ("I'm going to pick you up now"), but also that we pay attention to their non-verbal signals and listen to their sounds and cries. If we're unsure, we wait before reacting. We ask, give the child time to take our question in, and listen again. We make every attempt to understand what our babies might be communicating.

We won't always be successful in the beginning, but we'll improve with each try. Meanwhile our children hear our profoundly important message: "We want you to tell us what you need and feel. We believe you are capable of communicating with us, and we will do our best to understand you."

This is vital. Only we can open this door and wholeheartedly welcome our baby's communication.

2. Use your authentic voice and first person. Many believe in using "mother-ese", so I realize this is controversial, but here's what I've found... Talking to our babies in our regular, authentic voice (but a little slower) reminds us that we are talking to a whole person. It's easier and not as likely to induce headaches (which I know, because I talk to my dog in mother-ese). It models for babies the natural tone and language we want them to adopt. The more they hear language spoken properly, the sooner they will learn and try speaking it.

Children sense inauthenticity a mile away. The children I know who aren't used to being talked to in mother-ese feel disrespected and talked down to when adults speak to them this way.

Using first person rather than "Mommy loves Johnny" is a minor detail, but it is another way to remind

Janet Lansbury

ourselves to talk person-to-person with our baby. Why speak differently to a baby or toddler who is immersed in the process of learning our language than we would to an older child or adult? This makes no sense to me.

Never doubt for a moment that babies know who Mommy, Daddy and Johnny are. They don't need the constant reminders. Also, children understand and use pronouns earlier when they are modeled.

3. Talk about real, meaningful things. In other words, instead of teaching words, *use* them. Holding up a ball, pointing to it and saying "ball" is far less effective teaching than commenting in context on a relevant (and, therefore, meaningful) event. "You moved all the way to that red ball and touched it, and then it rolled further away."

Babies learn best, as we all do, when they care, and in this example the baby would probably care about his involvement with the words 'moved', 'red ball', 'touched', 'rolled' and 'away'. That's six words right there, but who's counting (aside from the experts…)?

Note: I'm not suggesting constant narration while babies play. The best way to gauge whether or not to comment while our child is engaged in an activity is to wait for him or her to communicate an interest in our response, which young children usually do by looking at us.

4. Read books and tell stories responsively. Reading books responsively means ditching any agenda and following the child's interest. Let the baby or toddler stay on one page for five minutes if she wants to and talk to her about everything you see there. Let her skip pages, look at the book upside down, and *not* finish the story (or even look at the book at all) if that's what she chooses. We encourage a love of books when we trust our child's readiness and allow reading to be child-led. And children who love books love and use language.

If you're the creative type (which I'm usually not at the end of the day), tell stories. I'll never forget the stories my dad told about Mary and her dog Zip. Actually, I don't remember anything specific about the stories themselves, but I thoroughly enjoyed that attention from my dad.

5. Slow down. I forget this all the time. We should probably put "Slow Down" signs all over the house when our children are small. There are so many good reasons to slow down around children, especially in regard to language. When we slow down, children can listen and understand.

6. Relax and be patient. Parent worries are usually felt by young children and don't create the ideal climate for taking big developmental strides. Talking takes courage. Relax, be patient and trust your child's inborn timetable. Many patient parents I know have experienced their child's verbal skills emerge overnight – a language "explosion".

If your child seems delayed in his or her ability to comprehend language, or seems atypical in several areas of development, get a professional assessment.

7. Don't test. What children need most of all to be able to start talking (or do just about anything else) is our trust. When we test, there is neither trust nor respect.

Magda Gerber's rule of thumb was: "Don't ask children a question you know the answer to." In other words, "Where is your nose?"

As excited as we get about sharing the adorable way our toddler pronounces his latest words ("Say 'turtle' for Grandma, Johnny!"), performance pressure makes toddlers more likely to clam up.

8. Babbling is talking. When babies or toddlers seem to be talking gibberish, they are usually saying words, so ignoring them or babbling back isn't as respectful or encouraging as saying, "You're telling me something. Are you telling me about the cat that just walked by?" Or, "You've got a lot to say today. "

Beware of these common language discouragers: corrections and invalidation.

Corrections: When children are trying out language, they are inclined to get colors, animals, and other things "wrong", and adults are inclined to correct these mistakes. Don't. It's unnecessary and discouraging. With our patience and modelling, toddlers will discern the difference between dogs and bears, red and orange, etc. soon enough.

In *Learning All the Time*, John Holt explains: "When children first learn to talk, they will often use the name of one object to refer to a whole class of similar objects."

In other words, when a toddler refers to every animal as a "dog", she isn't indicating that she doesn't know the difference, so correcting her is unnecessary, unwarranted and, arguably, disrespectful.

Holt offers this analogy: "If a distinguished person from a foreign country were visiting you, you would not correct every mistake he made in English, however much he might want to learn the language, because it would be rude. We do not think of rudeness or courtesy as being applicable to our dealings with very little children. But they are."

Invalidating thoughts and feelings: Let's say your toddler asks (in her unique way) to change her diaper, but you check and she isn't wet. Or maybe your boy says "lellon", and you know he loves melon, but he just ate. Rather than reflexively responding, "You don't need your diaper changed," or "You can't be hungry, you just ate", accept and acknowledge the communication without the slightest bit of judgment.

"Oh, are you saying you want to change your diaper?" (Wait for a response.) "Yes? Well, I can certainly understand wanting to do that again. It's fun to spend that time together. But you are dry and so we won't be changing you right now. Maybe in a few minutes."

"Are you thinking about melon?" (Wait for a response.) "Are you hungry for melon? (Wait.) Oh, you're not hungry? Are you enjoying saying "melon"? That's a fun word to say, isn't it?"

When we listen to and respect these early attempts at communication, children feel encouraged to keep talking. They'll sense that their most random thoughts, feelings and ideas are welcome to our ears. And chances are excellent we'll be their favorite confidant for many years to come.

(Note: if you have concerns about your child's language development, the American Academy of Pediatrics offers helpful guidelines on their web site.)

18.

Nurturing Creativity: How I Learned To Shut Up

Years ago, my two-and-a-half-year-old daughter was coloring Easter eggs. She had dipped an egg into the purple-dye cup and was about to blend it with yellow dye, when I stopped her. "You might not like the way those colors will look together," I warned. Willful girl that she's always been, she overruled me and proceeded to mix colors that I was certain would combine to look like a putrid shade of late-sixties shag rug.

To my amazement, her finished egg was indescribably beautiful. The luminous green-brown hue was unlike any I'd ever seen – glorious – beyond classification by any Benjamin Moore chart. And (to think!) my pedestrian Easter egg vision could have easily discouraged its existence.

The question – which came first, the chicken or the egg? — will always be a puzzle. But I feel certain that if the 'egg' represents a child's creative endeavors, a parent's trust must precede the egg. Trust in a child's instincts is the key to encouraging free access to her creative power.

Creativity is in all of us. It cannot be taught. It doesn't come in a craft kit, a toddler dance class, or in a parent's slew of brilliant ideas. Creative sparks happen, seemingly out of nowhere sometimes and often when we least expect them. They flow freer when undirected, certainly when un-judged.

Creative ideas come to me after a few minutes of running when my mind can wander. Sometimes they come to me in the shower, or in the semi-dream state I bask in when I first wake up before self-judgment has the opportunity to barge in with rights, wrongs, and self-doubt.

When we are babies, the lines of connectivity to our creative power are clear. We encourage our children to keep those lines open by being patient, accepting, providing lots of open-ended time for free play and choice, and most importantly, refraining from directing, judging either positively or negatively (both are perceived as judgment by a child) or otherwise interfering with our well-intentioned help.

Early Childhood educator and popular lecturer Bev Bos urged adults, "Never draw for a child." Her advice extends to include painting, sculpting, crafting, block tower and sand castle building, story creating, or anything artistic or creative.

When we show a child how to do those things, we intend to encourage creativity, but we interfere with it instead, by demonstrating for our child the 'right' way. We create doubt for our child in her abilities, and encourage our child's dependency on others to affirm for her what is 'right', or good. The artistic genius of a budding Picasso will persevere and overcome our influence, but we don't want to discourage *any* child from experimentation and the therapeutic benefits of the wide variety of creative outlets at her disposal.

Creativity comes to us naturally, but it takes courage to follow our intuition and express it. Whenever I write and publish something new, it feels like a leap from an airplane. Creative courage is shining a light in the darkness of boredom by dreaming up a new activity, or daring to fill blank space with our words or images. It is drawing a picture of a girl in bed "dreaming she is riding an elephant," as a 3 year-old I know did, even if no one else understood it (but if you looked closely, it was all there).

Einstein once said, "I believe in intuition and inspiration.... At times I feel certain I am right while not knowing the reason." Children are born with that conviction, but they are easily swayed by our doubt in their judgment and abilities.

We must be vigilantly aware of our children's powerful instinct to please us if we want them to keep trusting that voice inside. Some of us have to learn to shut up (as I did) so our children can continue to listen.

19.

'Sportscasting' Your Child's Struggles

Sportscasting (or 'broadcasting') is the term Magda Gerber coined to describe the nonjudgmental, "just the facts" verbalization of events she advised parents to use to support infants and toddlers as they struggle to develop new skills. Sportscasters don't judge, fix, shame, blame or get emotionally involved. They just keep children safe, observe and state what they see, affording children the open space they need to continue struggling until they either solve the problem or decide to let go and move on to something else:

"You're working very hard on fitting that puzzle piece. You seem frustrated."

"Savannah, you had the bear and now Ally has it. You both want to hold it. Savannah is trying to get it back... Ally, I won't let you hit."

"You're trying to climb back down from that step. I will keep you safe. I won't let you fall."

Here are five benefits of sportscasting:

1. When we do less, the children think and learn more. Surprisingly, these mini-commentaries are often all our children need to persevere with challenging tasks and resolve conflicts with siblings and peers. When more help is needed, we can transition into 'interview' mode by calmly asking open-ended questions like: "You both want that ball. What can you do?"

If struggles continue and feelings escalate, we might parse out a suggestion or two, like, "Did you notice there's another ball in that basket?" Or, "You might try placing just one foot down off that step first."

If the struggle is about physical play between two (or more) children and one of the children seems concerned, we can check-in by asking, "Is that okay with you?" If the child indicates that it's not, we might suggest, "You can say 'no' and move away" (and then we gently stop the action if necessary).

Less is always more.

RIE Parent/Toddler Guidance Classes typically end at around age two, but one of the classes I facilitate has chosen to remain together through the children's third year, so I've had the unique opportunity to practice sportscasting with preschoolers. Since these children are more verbal than the under-two's, I've been able to hone my 'interview' skills and been stunned by how well this approach still works. (Granted, these children are RIE-advantaged by having become accustomed to solving problems with minimal intervention.)

When the children are struggling over a toy, I sportscast and then ask: "Laura, what were you planning to do with that car?"

"I want to roll it down the ramp."

"Jake, you look upset. What do *you* want to do with the car?" He demonstrates that he wants to roll the car up the wall. "Oh, Jake wants to roll the car on the wall. Hmm. What can you two do?"

To my amazement, asking these three-year-olds to consider and express their desires is often all they've needed to resolve the struggle. The children end up deciding to either do the activities together, take turns and watch each other, or let go and move on to something else, all by themselves.

The temptation to lead, direct or solve problems can be great, but if we can control these impulses, children will learn much more and build confidence.

2. Trust empowers. Sportscasting is our most minimal conflict intervention tool and the most empowering, because it communicates trust and belief in our children. By sportscasting we are essentially saying, "I'm here and I support you, but I feel confident that you can handle this situation".

Sportscasters are not afraid of their children's age-appropriate feelings of loss, frustration, disappointment and anger. They patiently acknowledge those, too: "You are still so disappointed about that tower you were building. It's really upsetting to have it fall down."

We let whatever happens happen, and rather than creating for our children an unnecessary dependence on adults to fix situations for them, we foster resilience and self-confidence.

3. Reminds us not to judge or take sides. Sportscasting keeps our natural tendencies to judge or project in check. This is critical, because whenever we judge a child and/or her behavior we create shame, guilt and distance, which hinders our connection, undermines learning and self-confidence.

I'm so sensitive to projecting a problem where there isn't one or shaming children that I don't even like using the word 'took'. For me, there's a subtle, but important difference between, "You had that and now Tommy has it" and "Tommy *took* that from you."

Children often define 'play', 'fun' and 'problems' quite differently than adults do. I'll never forget the *one time* I tried to stick up for my son when he was on the receiving end of (what seemed to me) a relentless, over-the-top verbal blasting from his older sister. He pointed me to the door to "stay out of it". He's no masochist, so I can only assume he was enjoying himself.

By sportscasting we confirm our acceptance of the situation as is, which helps us to keep our eyes and minds open.

4. Encourages children not to identify as aggressors or victims. One of the biggest problems with responses that over-protect, shame or take sides is that the children involved can get stuck in the victim/aggressor roles we unwittingly assign them. Aggressors believe they are bad and mean. Victims feel weak and powerless. Both believe they are dependent on adults to intervene and solve their problems for them.

5. Provides children a clearer understanding of situations, teaches language, social and emotional intelligence. By sportscasting we facilitate experiential learning, which is education at its best, most meaningful and profound.

In some instances, sportscasting is *not* enough and a parent or care giver may have to intervene. For instance:

a) Safety issues – always our first priority.

b) Disruptive or destructive patterns of behavior. Children need gentle, firm reminders to not keep removing every toy from another child's hands, etc.

c) Children focused on a project should have their work protected if possible. But if we don't arrive in time to prevent a child from dismantling another child's project, we should still sportscast and interview.

Like all of the best child care practices, sportscasting works because it is about trusting our child's innate abilities -- and staying out of the way so she'll be empowered to use them.

20.

Toddlers and Sharing
(The S Word)

It's chanted on every playground and enforced at the park, parties and play dates. It's a word that has become the social mantra for parents of toddlers everywhere: *Share!*

We are all desperate for our children to share. Sharing is vital. The future of the world depends upon our children's spirit of generosity. We fear that if we don't remind our children to share, they might become selfish, stingy outcasts. Or perhaps we'll be judged indulgent, inconsiderate and ill-mannered parents.

The truth is that toddlers don't yet understand the concept of sharing, and our parental concerns make 'share' a loaded word. We tend to misuse it. We say, "Share", but what we really mean is, "Give what you have to another child."

Why would a child want to share his red truck when it means giving up the truck to someone else?

Toddlers want what they see, and that object becomes theirs. 'Mine' can mean either: I see it; I want it; or I'm using it. The idea of ownership — the concept that dad or mom bought an item at the store so now it belongs to them — is not entirely understood by a toddler.

It's common in RIE Parent/Infant Classes for children to want the same toy. The giving and taking of toys often begins as a social gesture, an infant's early attempt to make contact with another infant. The children may appear to be struggling with a toy, but with a bit of patience and objective observation, we usually see that there is little stress and lots of curiosity.

If a child reacts to the exchange with surprise or disappointment, Magda advised caregivers to sportscast rather than interfere. 'Sportscast' means to acknowledge the interactions of the children in a matter-of-fact way, never implying blame. Children often calm down when they feel that an adult understands. We might say, for example: "Rex, you were holding the car, and now Sophie has it." Or, "You and Sophie both want that toy."

There are no villains or victims in Toddlerland, just children learning by experimenting with social behaviors.

When infants and toddlers have opportunities for uninterrupted socialization, they will try out different options. Should they let go and allow the other child to take the ball away? What happens if they hold on tightly? If they do share or offer something to another child, how does that child react?

As Magda reminded us in her book *Your Self-Confident Baby*: "Self-learned lessons, whether sharing or the will to hold on, stick with us longer."

Children will often demonstrate that the interaction with another child is what interests them, not the toy itself. This is evident when there are multiples of a certain object available, yet the children are only interested in the one that has 'heat.' Soon after the struggle is over, the toy is usually dropped, becomes 'cold,' and no one wants it anymore. Children are best left to work these situations out by themselves while the adults insure that there is no hitting or hurting.

Many years ago I experienced the futility of adult interference in a toddler power struggle when I brought my daughter to her friend's house to play. The girls both wanted a particular doll. The girl's kind-hearted mother couldn't bear to see them fight, so she offered my daughter a replacement toy, a stuffed turtle. Of course, then both girls wanted the turtle, so she brought something else. She brought toy after toy to the girls, and they continued to fight over each new toy. Finally, after tears and yelling, the girls finished their rivalry, abandoned all the toys and went out in the yard to play, friends again.

So, how do we teach children to share with others?

1. Model generosity: For example, saying to a child, "You're reaching for my crackers. Here, I'll share some with you." Or, "Let's share this umbrella."

2. When our child demonstrates generosity, we acknowledge it: "It was kind of you to share those blocks with Robert."

3. Most importantly, we must be patient and trust that our child will learn to share in time.

No parent feels comfortable when their child takes from another, holds on to toys that another wants to use, or seems upset because another child will not share with him. But these situations usually look far worse from our point-of-view than they do from our child's.

When we unnecessarily intervene in a struggle by insisting that a child shares, we rob him of a social learning experience. When we insist that our child shares before he can truly understand what it means, we risk making 'share' a bad word.

A child shares when he begins to feel empathy for others, empathy modeled through a parent's patience and trust in him.

21.

The Trouble with Potty Training

Most of the conventional advice I hear about potty training is disappointing, to say the least. It usually focuses on no fuss 'tips and tricks' and boasts results in record time.

Shouldn't we have a little respect?

Potty training is not something we do *to* a child, or ask the child to do to please us. Children don't need to be manipulated with treats and rewards. It is a natural process that is best led completely by the child with our support.

Yes, I understand parents wondering, worrying and feeling impatient about successful toilet training, even though it is something every healthy normal child eventually achieves. But we can create resistance, distrust, even shame when we coax a child to the potty one moment before he's ready.

One problem is the word 'training,' which gives us the impression that we must be proactive in a process that is best advised to happen naturally. When children are ready, they train themselves. If we are patient and create the atmosphere of acceptance our child needs to initiate his transition from diapers to toilet, he will master the skill easily and gain the feeling of autonomy he deserves. Readiness is the key – physical, cognitive and emotional.

Physically: they must have bladder and bowel capacity and muscle control.

Cognitively: they must be fully aware of what they are supposed to do.

Emotionally: they must be emotionally ready to let go of a situation they are used to and comfortable with (urinating and releasing feces into a diaper whenever they feel like it).

Parents lay the groundwork for the child's readiness when, beginning at birth, we make diaper changes an enjoyable, cooperative time together and respect the baby by slowing down and talking him through each part of the process.

When the child begins to show signs of toilet readiness (he lets you know he has urinated; wants the wet diaper removed immediately; begins to tell you *before* he urinates), it might be time to have a small potty on hand. Then every person who cares for the child is advised to be on board to refrain from asking the child to use the potty, or nudging in anyway.

Some children are extremely sensitive to being pushed in this area, and reactions can be as extreme as holding feces in for days, or having to put a diaper on in order to have a bowel movement, even years after having been supposedly 'trained'.

I have seen cases where children began a pattern of resistance when the parent coaxed them to use the potty, and the relationship of resistance continued in other areas into adulthood. Parents must tread carefully when dealing with toilet issues.

It is safest to relax, remain patient and allow the child to tell us every time he wants to go to the toilet on his own. The process of self-training can take weeks, even months. Disruptions in the child's life (a new sibling, moving, traveling) can cause him to backtrack, even after we thought him fully trained. In those cases it's best to go with the flow (so to speak) and keep diapers or pull-ups available well after training seems finished.

Trusting our child pays off for everyone. The child takes pride in his newfound autonomy, and his self-confidence grows. By being trusted to 'let go' when he is ready, he can 'hold on' to intrinsic motivation. After all, if we have to control our bodily functions to please our parents, what can we ever own?

22.

No Bad Kids
Toddler Discipline without Shame

A toddler acting out is not shameful, nor is it behavior that needs punishing. It's a cry for attention, a shout-out for sleep, or a call to action for firmer, more consistent limits. It is the push-pull of your toddler testing his burgeoning independence. He has the overwhelming impulse to step out of bounds, while also desperately needing to know he is securely reined in.

There is no question that children need discipline. As infant expert Magda Gerber said, "Lack of discipline is not kindness, it is neglect."

The key to healthy and effective discipline is our attitude. Toddlerhood is the perfect time to hone parenting skills that will provide the honest, direct, and compassionate leadership our children will depend on for years to come. Here are some guidelines:

1. Begin with a predictable environment and realistic expectations. A predictable, daily routine enables a baby to anticipate what is expected of him. That is the beginning of discipline. Home is the ideal place for infants and toddlers to spend the majority of their day. Of course, we must take them with us to do errands sometimes, but we cannot expect a toddler's best behavior at dinner parties, long afternoons at the mall, or when his days are loaded with scheduled activities.

2. Don't be afraid or take misbehavior personally. When toddlers act out in my classes, the parents often worry that their child might be a brat, a bully, or an aggressive kid. When parents project those fears, it can cause the child to internalize the negative personas, or at least pick up on the parent's tension, which often exacerbates the misbehavior.

Instead of labeling a child's action, learn to nip the behavior in the bud by disallowing it nonchalantly. If your child throws a ball at your face, try not to get annoyed. He doesn't do it because he dislikes you, and he's not a bad child. He is asking you (toddler-style) for the limits that he needs and may not be getting.

3. Respond in the moment, calmly, like a CEO. Finding the right tone for setting limits can take a bit of practice. Lately, I've been encouraging parents that struggle with this to imagine they are a successful CEO and that their toddler is a respected underling. The CEO corrects the errors of others with confident, commanding efficiency. She doesn't use an unsure, questioning tone, get angry or emotional.

Our child needs to feel that we are not nervous about his behavior or ambivalent about establishing rules. He finds comfort when we are effortlessly in charge.

Lectures, emotional reactions, scolding and punishments do not give our toddler the clarity he needs and can create guilt and shame. A simple, matter-of-fact "I won't let you do that, if you throw that again I will take it away," while blocking the behavior with our hands, is the best response. But react immediately. Once the moment has passed, it is too late. Wait for the next one!

4. Speak in first person. Parents often get in the habit of calling themselves "mommy" or "daddy". Toddlerhood is the time to change over into first person for the most honest, direct communication possible. Toddlers test boundaries to clarify the rules. When I say "Mommy doesn't want Emma to hit the dog", I'm not giving my child the direct ('you' and 'me') interaction she needs.

5. No time-out. I always think of Magda Gerber asking in her grandmotherly Hungarian accent, "Time out of what - time out of life?"

Magda was a believer in straightforward, honest language between a parent and child. She didn't believe in gimmicks like 'time-out', especially to control a child's behavior or to punish him. If a child misbehaves in a public situation, the child is usually indicating he's tired, losing control and needs to leave.

Carrying a child to the car to go home, even if he kicks and screams, is the respectful way to handle the issue. Sometimes a child has a tantrum at home and needs to be taken to his room to flail and cry in our presence until he regains self-control. These are not punishments, but caring responses.

6. Consequences. A toddler learns discipline best when he experiences natural consequences for his behavior, rather than a disconnected punishment like time-out. If a child throws food, mealtime is over. If a child refuses to get dressed, we don't go to the park today. These parental responses appeal to a child's sense of fairness. The child may still react negatively to the consequence, but he does not feel manipulated or shamed.

7. Don't discipline a child for crying. Children need rules for behavior, but their emotional responses to the limits we set (or to anything else, for that matter) should be allowed, even encouraged.

Toddlerhood can be a time of intense, conflicting feelings. Children may need to express anger, frustration, confusion, exhaustion and disappointment, especially if they don't get what they want because we've set a limit. A child needs the freedom to safely express his feelings without our judgment. He may need a pillow to punch — give him one.

8. Unconditional love. Withdrawing our affection as a form of discipline teaches a child that our love and support turns on a dime, evaporating because of his momentary misbehavior. How can that foster a sense of security?

Alfie Kohn's 2009 *New York Times* article "When A Parent's 'I Love You' Means 'Do As I Say'" explores the damage this kind of conditional parenting causes -- the child grows to resent, distrust and dislike his parents, feels guilt, shame, and a lack of self-worth.

9. Spanking – NEVER. Most damaging of all to a relationship of trust are spankings. And spanking is a predictor of violent behavior. In her article "The Long-

Term Effects of Spanking" Alice Park reports findings from a recent study that point to "...the strongest evidence yet that children's short-term response to spanking may make them act out more in the long run. Of the nearly 2,500 youngsters in the study, those who were spanked more frequently at age 3 were much more likely to be aggressive by age 5."

Purposely inflicting pain on a child cannot be done with love. Sadly, however, the child often learns to associate the two.

Loving our child does not mean keeping him happy all the time and avoiding power struggles. Often it is doing what feels hardest for us to do: saying "no" and meaning it.

Our children deserve our direct, honest responses so they can internalize right and wrong and develop the authentic self-discipline needed to respect and be respected by others. As Magda wrote in *Dear Parent – Caring for Infants With Respect*: "The goal is inner-discipline, self-confidence and joy in the act of cooperation."

23.

Struggling With Boundaries (3 Common Reasons)

One of the most disappointing things I hear from parents I consult with is that they aren't enjoying parenting, especially when it comes to setting limits, which has become a source of confusion and often guilt. What's most concerning to them is that they sense their children aren't happy either. It's usually because they're both confused about boundaries.

These are parents who will never need to worry about being overly strict – it simply isn't in their constitution. Like me years ago, they are drawn to Magda Gerber's parenting approach and her recommendations to respect babies as whole people, trust their intrinsically motivated development, and encourage their self-directed free play.

Trust, empathy and unconditional love seem to come naturally for parents like us -- boundaries, not so much.

It can be easy for us to become so focused on giving our children trust and freedom that we overlook their even more crucial need to feel securely rooted. Too much freedom actually makes our children feel the *opposite* of free, and they often express their discomfort through limit-pushing behavior.

To experience true freedom and happiness, kids need gentle leaders who are clear about house rules and expectations. They need a healthy balance between freedom and boundaries.

In my work with parents over the last twenty years (and as a parent myself), I've noted some of the most common reasons many of us struggle to find this balance:

We'd prefer not to upset our children. Who would? Discomfort with our children's strong emotions is the number one reason parents struggle to provide clear boundaries and can cause us to question or doubt every decision we might make:

Hmmm, I guess I could carry my five-year-old down the street after all, even though my back is aching.

Why not just give him back the blue cup? So what if he screamed, "No, I want green!" and then changed his mind again? Sure, I'm annoyed, but it would be so easy to try one more time to please him.

Since I'm really in no hurry, I might as well wait another fifteen minutes for her to decide she's ready get into her car seat.

Our children's age-appropriate resistance and intensely emotional reactions to our boundaries can make us feel guilty and worried, wear us out, ruin our whole day. For limit-setting to work and for parents to enjoy (read: survive) the toddler years, getting used to this basic dynamic is essential: *We confidently establish a boundary. Our child expresses displeasure (which can include frustration, disappointment, sadness, anger, rage). We stay anchored during this storm, patiently accepting and acknowledging our child's displeasure.*

Children often push our boundaries because they know intuitively that they need the safety of our calm, confident responses, and also to offload uncomfortable feelings simmering inside them. Our acceptance of these feelings eases the need to test and is one of the most profound ways we can express our love. It gets a little easier for us with practice.

Confusing advice. Lately I've been disappointed by advice I'm reading from non-punitive parenting experts, especially when I notice how misleading, confusing and discouraging these suggestions are for the parents reaching out to me. For instance:

a) *"Only set limits with your children for safety reasons."*

This is a formula for insecure children and miserable parents. What about emotional safety and peace of mind – the relief of knowing that we're not expected to call all the shots when we're only two years old? And does this mean parents don't have rights to their personal boundaries and self-care?

b) *"Don't set limits that might feel like punishments to your children."*

This one could get us questioning ourselves all day long because it plays right into our doubts and fears about upsetting our children. As respectful parents courageously committed to non-punitive discipline, we need to grant ourselves permission to make the decisions we deem best for us and our children.

Yes, it's okay to move to another room if our child won't stop screaming, even if they find that upsetting. Yes, it's okay to say honestly, "We won't be able to leave for the park until you help me pick these toys", or "Please come brush your teeth now, so we'll have time for an extra book", or "I see you want to play with the folded laundry, but I don't want it unfolded on the floor, so I'm going to pick this basket up. Here's an empty one you can use."

If we decide later that a decision we've made is unfair or unnecessary, we can always apologize and change our minds. But to foster a sense of security for our children we must make these decisions from a platform of strength rather than hesitancy. To be gentle leaders with self-confident children, we must first trust ourselves.

c) *"When children push limits, make them laugh."*

I believe it is asking way too much to suggest that we take the annoyance (or worse) we feel when children push our limits and turn that into games and laughter.

Yet this is exactly what some gentle, non-punitive parenting experts advise us to try first, even in response to our kids' aggressive behaviors like hitting and biting. I see so many problems with this advice I don't know where to begin.

First, it isn't beneficial to us or our children to pretend to feel silly and perky when we are actually annoyed or angry. Shouldn't we be modelling authenticity? And doesn't this teach children that their negative feelings are not okay? They should laugh when they're angry? Second, what if our children's behavior angers or enrages us? Is this a healthy time to be rough-housing, tickling, blowing raspberries on our kids? Not in my experience.

Ironically, these are the experts who also purportedly advocate for allowing children to express their strong feelings, but rather than help normalize this challenging experience for parents, their advice is essentially saying, "Only let your children cry as a last resort. Do a song and dance first and get 'em laughing if you can."

We are afraid our limits might crush our child's free spirit. Truly, this works exactly the other way around. Over the years in my classes, I've worked with many parents who have had difficulties setting limits. When they eventually figure this out and make changes, the transformations in their children's behavior and demeanor are dramatic. Formerly clingy and demanding children are suddenly able to stop trying to control every situation with parents or peers. They are able to focus on play, socialize with their peers, participate in snack time, loosen up enough to laugh and express joy.

This is freedom.

24.

What Your Toddler Thinks of Discipline

I've been told that I "understand" toddlers (and nothing could be a greater compliment). This might be because my own emotional development was partially arrested as a toddler for reasons I haven't yet unraveled. It's probably also because after all the time I've spent observing toddlers, I've begun to identify with them.

Sometimes, for example, when a parent in class asks her toddler not to throw toys, I'll be unconvinced by her delivery and feel like joining the toddler in throwing more toys. Other times a child will say he wants to leave the class as soon as he's arrived. I'll feel the toddler's edginess while the parent is thinking, "Uh-oh, now what?" or is afraid to take a stand. The toddler will persist with the issue until his parent says decisively, "I hear you wanting to leave, but we won't be going until class ends."

If toddlers could share their thoughts on discipline, here's what I think they'd say...

Make me your ally. Don't think in terms of "getting me to do" something. Don't trick, bribe, shame or punish me. You-against-me is scary when I desperately need you on my side.

So please tell me politely or show me what you want. And stop me kindly (but definitively) from doing things you don't want - and way before you get mad.

Your calm demeanor and the positive options you give me ("I see you're playing, so would you like to come in to change your diaper now or after you play for 5 more minutes?") will help me to accept your instructions more gracefully.

Don't be afraid of my reactions to limits. It's discomforting for me when you are timid, tentative or evasive. How can I ever feel secure if the people I desperately need to depend on waver or tiptoe around my feelings?

So please put periods at the end of your sentences and then calmly accept my displeasure. Your directions are more welcome than you'll ever know. They don't hurt my fragile spirit. They free me, help me enormously and are essential to my happiness.

Tell me the truth in simple terms so that I can feel very clear about what you want. I may need several reminders while I'm learning, so please be patient and try to stay even-toned, even if you've already told me. (Really, I don't want to be annoying.)

Don't get upset or angry if you can possibly help it. Those reactions don't make me feel safe. I need to know that my behavior doesn't get to you, that you can handle my issues with care and confidence. If not you, then who?

If I keep repeating the behavior, it's because it doesn't feel resolved for me. Either you aren't being convincing enough, or you're being too intense and emotional. When you give me "the look", or there's anger in your voice when you say, "Don't hit!" it unnerves me, and I'm compelled to keep behaving that way until you can give me a calmer response.

I need to know that those kinds of behaviors aren't allowed, but I also need to be assured constantly that they are no big deal at all and can be easily handled by you. You'll show me this by being patient, calm, consistent and giving me brief, respectful, direct responses so that we can both let go and move on, knowing that our connection is still solid.

Consider my point of view and acknowledge it as much as possible...even if it seems ridiculous or wrong. There are no wrong desires or feelings, just wrong ways of acting on them, right? I need to know that it's okay to have these feelings and that you'll understand and keep on loving me. Let me feel.

Remember that I don't want to be in charge, even though the toddler creed is to never admit that. I am convincing. I can make you believe that your simple request to sit down while I eat is pure torture. Don't mock me or call me out, but don't believe it. Keep insisting — with love. My strong will is going to make you proud someday. When you give in all the time, I feel less strong, far more wobbly.

Give me lots of 'yes' time when I have your full attention and appreciation for all the good stuff I do. We all need balance.

Let me be a problem solver. If our wishes are at odds, consider me capable of helping to find a solution, especially as I get older.

Thank you for doing all of these really, really, really hard things in order to help me be the kind of kid who is enjoyed by his friends, is welcome in their parents' homes, appreciated by teachers, and is (most of all) one of your favorite people to be with in the whole wide world...forever.

25.

Toddler Discipline That Works

The secret to raising children who generally cooperate with our rules and direction has very little to do with specific strategies or wordplay like "I won't let you" versus "Don't hit."

What matters most — and essentially makes or breaks successful guidance — is the way we perceive our children and our overall attitude toward boundaries and discipline. The good news is that once these perceptions are on-track we can make lots of mistakes, and yet we'll almost never go wrong.

Treat them like people: Two decades ago I was invited to attend the introductory session of a parenting seminar led by Mary Hartzell, a highly respected author and preschool director. I remember little about Mary's lecture except that I agreed with her approach. What I recall vividly is that when it came time for questions, a flood of fervent questions poured forth from the audience, and they all began: "How do I get my child to...?"

Parents wanted to *get* their preschoolers to brush teeth, pick up toys, toilet train, or leave the park. They wanted to *get* them to stop hitting, pushing, biting, spitting, etc. It was clear from the tone of their questions, especially the repeated use of the word "get", that many were on the wrong track.

They were approaching these issues with an "us and them" attitude rather than a teamwork mentality. They were looking for quick fixes, tricks and manipulation tactics instead of working person-to-person and building the kind of trusting, mutually respectful relationship that makes discipline (and every other aspect of parenting) much simpler and more rewarding.

Of course, I doubt that I would have recognized this had I not been fresh out of my training with infant specialist Magda Gerber.

A few days after the lecture, I ran into the friend who had invited me and expressed my appreciation. He raved, "Mary is wonderful. She has helped us so much. The amazing thing she taught us was to *talk* to our 3-year-old about our expectations just like I would talk to you… just like we would speak to any other person."

"Sounds great!" I replied. "Magda Gerber teaches us to do that with babies." My friend's expression froze, and he looked puzzled, as if perhaps he'd misheard me. "Really?" he asked, eyes glazing over. And then we both dropped it. It didn't seem the time to try to explain.

Babies are sentient, aware people from the moment they are born; ready to begin an honest, communicative relationship with us. Through our respectful relationship, children of all ages are far more inclined to listen and cooperate.

On the other hand, trying to *get* the people in our lives to do the things we want them to do seldom works more than once or twice, and it doesn't make us like each other or really teach anything (except perhaps mistrust).

Presenting ourselves as the gentle leader that guides, models, demonstrates, coaches, and *helps* our children to behave appropriately is the key to discipline.

Redefine quality time: The way I see it, parents have to wear two hats: a *party hat* and a *professional hat*. When we're wearing our party hat, we're enjoying our kids, feeling connected, loving and fun. It's easy to recognize this as quality time.

Wearing the professional hat is not so much fun, but it does not have to be excruciating either. I implore the parents I work with to re-imagine quality time to include those moments when we are calmly, but assuredly facing our child's resistance to his or her bedtime routine; firmly preventing our baby from hitting the dog; or patiently removing our children from situations when they've lost all control so they can melt down safely in our presence.

Meltdowns and setting limits = quality time? What?! I know it's counterintuitive, but from our children's perspective, I feel certain it's true.

The times we must wear our professional hat are perhaps the most precious kind of quality time, because children need our empathetic leadership even more than they need us to be their playmates and most ardent fans. I truly believe that our kids sense how difficult it is for us to wear this hat gracefully, and they will test our limits to see if they can knock it off (the hat, that is).

Embracing the idea that this professional time is also quality time is especially crucial for working parents, or those with multiple children, or parents who (for whatever reason) don't have as much time to spend with their children as they would like, either routinely or just on that particular day.

Of course, we'd all prefer to spend the little time we have together joyously, but quite often that is not the dynamic our children need from us. They need to be able to complain, resist, stomp their feet, cry, and express their darker feelings with the assurance that they have our acceptance and acknowledgment. They need to know that they have a leader who will help them to comply with rules and boundaries in the face of their "no's" and not be intimidated by their displeasure and disagreement.

They need parents who can be capable leaders (so capable that we actually make it look easy), not just Good Time Charlies, people who they sense deep down have their very best interests, health and good character in mind.

One of my biggest aspirations as an educator is to effect change in our perceptions of discipline, boundaries and limits — to help transform these terms from negative to positive. Boundaries and discipline, when offered non-punitively and in the context of empathy and respect, are gifts we should feel proud of and one of the highest forms of love.

Once this is recognized, I'm convinced that parents and children will struggle far less and enjoy each other much more.

26.

Let Your Kids Be Mad At You

I always write from personal experience, though I am rarely the protagonist. This story is especially personal and, honestly, it feels a bit risky to share, but it's important so I'm taking the plunge...

I had the perfect mom. We adored each other and had a wonderful relationship right up until her death four and a half years ago. She loved to laugh and make others laugh, and everyone who knew her relished her company — her children and grandchildren most of all. She was perpetually and reliably loving and supportive. I always felt she was in my corner and my biggest fan.

My mom had only one major flaw: she talked on the phone. How *could* she ignore us for those ten or fifteen minutes? Oh, and occasionally she went to the bathroom and closed the door (the nerve!). Otherwise my mom was absolutely, incredibly perfect, and I will always, always think so.

Then there was me. I remember a mostly happy childhood, yet it was evident early on that I lacked confidence. Even though I had lot going for me on the outside, I don't ever remember feeling entirely comfortable in my own skin, the way the children I work with and my own children clearly do.

In my late teens, as my public career began to flourish, my insecurities really took root. Part of my job as an actress was appearing forever cheerful and 'on' at parties, publicity events and on the set, all of which I managed relatively gracefully. Deep down, though, I was dying. It was the 80's, so of course I did my share of drinking and drugging, which had the effect of helping me to feel some false confidence and a comfort that I'd never really experienced before.

I'll fast-forward through the details, but suffice it to say that at 25 I was an emotional time bomb. When I finally slowed down enough take stock and face my demons, I was flooded by the feelings I'd been avoiding and stuffing away all those years. I wasn't prepared for the accompanying anxiety, or especially the self-loathing and depression, never mind the panic attacks. I was a mess, and for a long time I cried from morning 'til night. I cried a river... and I actually think this is what helped to heal me.

After a few years of very intense work on myself, I slowly, slowly began the process of self-forgiveness and acceptance.

But what was so wrong with me?

This whole experience seems especially bizarre to me now that I have a 21-year old who could not be more different than I was at her age. Like my other two children, she is grounded, secure, capable and self-confident.

So, again, what was the matter with me?

I got an inkling several years later, and this brings me back to my mother. By then I was happily married with two kids. I was having my daily phone conversation with my mom when she made a comment (in jest, I'm sure) that I objected to a bit. There was an old joke in my family that I was useless in the kitchen. This was certainly based on fact, had been true for most of my life, and I had always happily played along with it.

But since becoming a mom I'd changed a lot. I'd become the responsible person I needed to be. I'd figured out how to cook for myself and my family. I didn't feel that I deserved the label "pathetic-in-the-kitchen" anymore.

So although I'm certain I didn't even raise my voice (because I had never raised my voice to my mother so long as I can remember), my feelings were hurt, and I got a little defensive. I objected to her comment.

She hung up on me. I called her back, but she didn't respond. I tried again...and again. I left messages, but she wouldn't speak to me. It took five days, and for those five days my anxiety was through the roof. I couldn't breathe. I was in a constant state of panic. And strangely, deep within me I *knew* this place...it was familiar. I don't remember when or how, but I knew I'd felt this terror before.

Eventually my mom took my call...and neither of us ever mentioned what had happened. I was so grateful and relieved to be breathing again that I would not have dreamed of saying anything that might drive my mother away from me.

My dear mom had never laid a hand on me, never punished me, and never yelled. But she clearly could not handle my feelings. The result was that I felt innately bad and wrong for ever having them.

So I've made a special effort to accept all my children's emotions, especially their anger...to let them know that it's always okay for them to be mad at me. I'm not going anywhere.

I've been far from perfect, but the good news is that with kids, we *do* get points for trying, especially if we confront and repair our mistakes. "I'm sorry I lost my patience."

We are human, and our kids are incredibly forgiving.

27.

An Easily Forgotten Gift

"Oh, Mama, just look at me one minute as though you really saw me."
— Thornton Wilder, *Our Town*

I know the gift all children want most — we all want it — but it's a hard one to remember. I've forgotten it for days, even weeks at a time. Sometimes it takes a desperate situation to remind me.

Several years ago my independent ten-year-old went through a phase during which she saw no reason to bathe. Days would pass. She would come up with excuses. I would let her off the hook and then forget about it. Finally, the time came when I knew I must force the issue, but I was still hesitant to demand it. Bathing should be looked forward to as a pleasant experience, not dreaded as an angry and resentful one.

Luckily for me, the Good Parent Fairy whispered Magda Gerber's magic words to me -- "pay attention" - and I was reminded of her thoughts on baby "caregiving".

Magda directed parents to give full attention to babies when feeding, diapering, bathing and at bedtime. Rather than treating these activities as unpleasant chores and rushing through them, Magda taught us to take advantage of intimate moments together by slowing down and including the baby in each step.

When we do these activities *with*, rather than *to* a baby, we cultivate a relationship based on respect and trust. Daily intervals of focused attention refuel children, giving them the nurturing they need to spend time playing independently.

When our babies get older, caregiving opportunities are not as delineated. They might look like: removing a splinter; putting make-up on a bar-mitzvah-bound daughter; or lying with a son at bedtime while he sobs about an unkind playmate. Even though my daughter was fully capable of bathing herself, it was worth a shot to see if she needed my attention. So, I asked her, "Shall I wash your hair for you in the bath? " "Yeah... okay," she answered meekly. Bingo.

Would you rather have close proximity to a busy loved one all day long, or a few minutes of that loved one's undivided attention?

Our children need real attention more than they need video games, iPods and trips to Disneyland. Focused attention is the glue that holds relationships together. Please excuse my Hallmark sentimentality, but *simple moments of true togetherness, whether we are happy or sad, mean the most.*

Then why is it so hard to remember?

My newborn son had colic. He would wake in the night several times and cry for an hour or more before I could get him back to sleep. I was an exhausted mess. And my two daughters were processing the new addition to the family.

My four-year-old exhibited the expected mood swings: Adoring her brother and being supportive of me one minute, then whining and crying the next. She was in obvious mourning for the loss of her previous life -- life without a baby that took up most of her mom's time and energy.

My nine-year-old daughter was a perfect angel, which, if I'd been paying attention, should have been a giant red flag. She made no demands of me, stayed out of my way and off my radar. I deliriously thought, "She's old enough to understand this situation. She's fine." My husband and I had heard a glowing report about her in a teacher conference before the baby's birth. She has always been an excellent student, but she was not without her difficult moments at home. Children are inclined to give those they are closest to (and feel safest with) the backhanded compliment of their worst behavior.

A few weeks after the baby was born, we got a phone call from the nine-year-old's teacher. Our daughter had begun acting out in class. She had talked back to the assistant teacher and stuck her tongue out. Displaying a rebellious attitude at school was totally uncharacteristic. My heart sank. I realized that my older daughter must not have felt 'safe' to act out with her overwhelmed mom. So, instead, for the first time ever she was showing her worst to the outside world.

That day after school, I sat in the car with her and talked. I asked about her feelings, imploring her to express anger, sadness, loss, all the thoughts she must have felt the need to keep from me. I suggested the feelings she might be having, and how normal, how expected they all would be. She could not answer, except for once or twice saying quietly, "I don't know."

I became desperate for her to respond. I was in tears then, but still nothing. This one-way dialogue went on for thirty or forty minutes, but it felt like hours. I was beside myself. Just as I was about to give up and return with her to the house, my usually strong, assertive daughter spoke in a tiny, pained voice. "Pay attention to me."

From then on I made a concerted effort to let my daughter know that I could handle anything she might need to throw my way. I carved out a little bit of time each day just for her. When she saw that I was not too overwhelmed to be there for her bright and dark sides, her behavior at school returned to normal. I was grateful to her teacher (who, interestingly, has always been my daughter's favorite) for alerting us to a change in our daughter immediately.

In hindsight, I think of those times my parental presence was needed – for issues large or small, important or mundane, joyous or heart-wrenching – as the most cherished moments in my life. Giving real attention has always turned out to be a gift to me, too.

28.

I Think I Know Why You're Yelling

"I find that I become one of two moms when my children are upset. I'm either Mary Poppins — kind, loving, patient — or I'm completely intolerant and prone to yelling and screaming."

- A Concerned Mom

If you're yelling at your kids, you're not alone. In fact, my own empirical research suggests yelling has become something of a parenting epidemic. Some are even calling it "the new spanking".

Why are so many dedicated, intelligent, aware parents losing control?

My sense is that parents often end up yelling because they've actually made the very *positive* decision to give their children boundaries with respect rather than punishments and manipulation. These parents are working really hard to remain gentle and kind, and yet their children's testing behaviors continue. They become increasingly frustrated, even fearful, feeling they've lost all control without any way to rein in their children.

And it's no wonder! If I attempted to absorb all the vague, contradictory advice I've seen and heard regarding discipline, I'd be blowing a gasket on a regular basis myself. So many of these theoretical ideas are seductively warm and fuzzy, but they come with a whole lot of scary *don'ts* ("don't punish, reward, control, give time-outs or consequences, use the word 'no', expect obedience, be authoritative, etc"), and very little in the way of practical tools.

If you've been yelling, here are some thoughts to consider:

1. You aren't taking care of yourself. A long soak in a warm tub or getting away with friends or your spouse are always good ideas, but what I'd suggest is far more basic and crucial: know your limits and personal needs, and establish boundaries with your child from the beginning. Yes, even with your infant.

For example, in the context of a respectful relationship (which means perceiving your infant as a whole person and communicating with her as such), it is okay for your baby to cry for a few minutes while you make your regular morning trip to the bathroom to brush your teeth. You leave your baby in a safe, enclosed place, tell her you will go and always acknowledge her feelings when you return.

Since you are respecting your baby's need for predictability, you've made this activity a habitual part of your day together, and your baby learns to anticipate that you will go and return. She still may complain, which is her right, but you confidently let her know you hear her and accept her expression of displeasure. "You didn't want me to go. That upset you. I'm back."

If you are a sensitive person who can't sleep deeply with your baby near you, but you're co-sleeping because you think you should, *you are not taking care of yourself.*

If you want to wean your child or limit your toddler's nursing, but you feel guilty about that, *you are not taking care of yourself.*

If you need to go to the kitchen to make a cup of coffee, but you're afraid to leave your fussy baby or screeching toddler, *you are not taking care of yourself.*

In fact, if you feel guilty about any self-care moment, *you are probably not taking care of yourself.*

We all give up much of our lives for our children, but it is unhealthy for us (and even less healthy for our kids) to become an egoless parent, neglecting our needs and virtually erasing ourselves from the relationship. We need personal boundaries, and our children need us to model them. This is what it means to have an honest, authentic, respectful relationship that will make limit-setting in the toddler-through-teenage years clear and simple. (Notice I didn't say "easy" — because it's hardly ever easy.)

Parenting fact: Our babies and toddlers will never give us permission to take care of our needs. "Go ahead and take a little break, mom, you deserve it!" will never be said or implied through our young children's behavior, even on Mother's Day. Quite the opposite, in fact. These boundaries must come from *us,* and our children will do their job by objecting, rebelling, making demands and more demands, and continuing to feel around for our limits until they are firmly and consistently in place.

2. You have spent your baby's first year distracting, appeasing or otherwise manipulating her rather than speaking honestly about limits. It disappoints me to hear some of the non-punitive discipline advocates I admire making statements like this one: "The bad news is that babies often want everything they see. The good news is that they're generally distractible during the first year."

Your baby is a whole person ready to engage actively and honestly in a relationship with you at birth. When you distract, you are practicing *avoidance* – denying an honest connection in order to side-step your child's healthy feelings of resistance.

The pattern this creates for both of you will make it so much harder for you to feel comfortable setting respectful limits later on. This formative first year is a crucial time to set limits honestly, because this is when we will establish what will always be the core of our parent/child relationship.

3. You feel responsible for your children's emotions. Here are the main reasons parents neglect to establish personal boundaries with their children or use manipulative tools like distraction (all of which often lead to yelling):

a) They don't believe a baby is really a whole person who can understand words and interact honestly.

b) They can't make peace with the discomfort they feel surrounding their child's emotions.

c) They perceive all crying as something to avoid or fix, "one-note communication", rather than a nuanced dialogue.

d) They ride the whirlwind of their child's disappointment, sadness, anger, etc. rather than being an anchor with the understanding that it is essential to emotional health for children to express themselves.

This unhealthy perception of children and their feelings thwarts the development of emotional resiliency, creates the need for even more limit-setting in the toddler years, and will exhaust you every time you have to say 'no' or insist upon something (which will be often).

The toddler years, especially, are a limit-pushing, resistant period. Your child *needs* to behave this way in order to individuate in a healthy manner. If you feel pained about or responsible for your child's daily roller-coaster of emotions, you're going to be reluctant to set honest limits, get tired, and probably end up yelling...or crying, which isn't healthy for your children either.

Repeat after me: *Once I've fulfilled my child's basic needs, my only responsibility regarding feelings is to accept and acknowledge them.*

4. Your expectations are unreasonable. You also might be yelling because you are expecting the impossible. Children are explorers. They need safe places where they can freely move, experiment, investigate. Asking a toddler not to run, jump or climb is akin to saying, "Don't breathe."

Create and find safe places for your children to play. Don't expose them to materials or equipment they can't use as they wish and thereby set yourself up for frustration and anger when they don't comply.

It's up to us to avoid situations that will try our patience rather than get caught up struggling to keep the peace and make it work.

5. You are confused about setting limits gently with respect. Join the club. My previous chapter in this book "No Bad Kids – Toddler Discipline Without Sharme" has lots of suggestions.

6. You needlessly enter into power struggles. It takes two to struggle, so don't engage. You are not your child's peer; you are her capable leader. So instead of taking your child's healthy, age-appropriate button-pushing behavior personally and going to that "uh-oh" place that leads you to yelling:

a) Make eye contact with your child and confidently state a limit: "It's time to brush your teeth."

b) Give a simple choice or opportunity for an autonomous decision: "If you can come now, we'll have time for a second book."

c) Acknowledge your child's feelings of disagreement (and welcome those feelings to continue as long as they need to, while you continue to acknowledge them). "Oh, I know you are having so much fun with the dog and it's hard to stop, but it's time. What a bummer! You are really upset and disappointed that it's bedtime. I know the feeling."

As *completely* counterintuitive as this is for most of us, it works. The more you are willing to agree with your child's feelings while calmly holding on to the boundary, the easier it will be for her to release her resistance and move on. How can your child continue to fight when you won't stop agreeing with her? This parenting "white-flag" of empathy will miraculously dissolve the tension for both of you.

d) If your child still does not comply for whatever reason, follow through by taking her hand (literally or figuratively). "You're having a hard time coming upstairs to brush your teeth, so I'm going to help you." You calmly take her hand, and then perhaps you add, "Thank you for letting me know you needed help."

This, by the way, is exactly what she was doing. And once you've recognized that *all* of your child's resistant, impulsive, objectionable behavior is really just an awkward request for your help, you'll probably find it easier to stop yelling about it.

29.

Never Too Late For Respectful Parenting

Since most of the advice I share is focused on the infant, toddler and preschool years, parents who have older children frequently ask me, "Is it too late?"

My answer is an unqualified, "Never."

The follow-up question is: "Great, so how do I begin?"

I answer that by sharing some of the ways Magda Gerber's Educaring Approach (RIE) has continued to inform my parenting with my own children, now 21, 17 and 12:

Keeping faith in our kids' competency: RIE's first principle is about having basic trust in infant competence. Belief in our kids as capable, whole people is a self-fulfilling prophecy that fosters tremendous self-confidence and the healthiest parent-child dynamic imaginable.

When we begin with trust, our children have opportunities to *show* us that they are able to figure out life's challenges like walking, talking, climbing, how toys work, toilet learning, reading, relationships, homework, eventually applying to college, etc. Through these autonomous struggles and accomplishments our trust in their abilities grows along with their self-confidence.

Alternatively, if we don't truly believe our kids are capable of handling age-appropriate tasks without our assistance, or we worry that they'll be crushed by frustration, mistakes, disappointments or failures, we might perpetuate a cycle of dependency.

For example, the need some teenagers seem to have to be prodded or nagged to do their homework has often been created by parents who believe children *need* them to nag to get the job done. Putting an end to a cycle like this one entails stepping back and letting go, having faith in our child to cope with age-appropriate situations, and allowing the issue of completing homework to be worked out where it should be — between children and their teachers.

Practicing basic trust as children grow means intervening as minimally as possible:

a. Whenever children have choices, let *them* choose — trust children's individual learning agendas rather than imposing ours on them.
b. Honor each child's unique developmental process rather than focusing on results, accomplishments, milestones.
c. Calmly support children through their frustration, disappointment and even failure, so that we normalize these difficult but healthy life experiences.
d. Let kids do it their way, even if we might believe ours is better.

Encouraging inner-directedness and 'process': If we allow them to, children will remind us of the importance of *now* and impart other affirming messages like: less is more; simple is best; earlier is not better; life is not a race; the joy is in the journey.

But rather than be inspired, many parents mistakenly believe it's their job to help their kids get ahead, so they stimulate, teach, place them in enrichment classes every day after school, and fill their weekends with exciting activities and events. These parents might not realize that children actually learn best when they do less and have more time to digest, integrate and assimilate their experiences.

"... But the child does not want to get anywhere; he just wants to walk, and to help him truly the adult must follow the child, and not expect him to keep up."
                    - Maria Montessori, *Education for a New World*

How do we discern enough stimulation from too much? Again, the answer will always be *trust*. To raise inner-directed, passionate kids we must encourage them to listen to the quiet voice inside them, the one only they can hear and that parents can easily drown out. Begin with an enriching home environment and let children clearly indicate their need for more. And don't over-praise, so your children's journeys and accomplishments can continue to be self-rewarding.

Accepting children's feelings without judging or rushing them: Letting our kids express intense feelings is one of our biggest challenges, because most of us weren't encouraged to do this by our own parents. We might have been told that our outbursts were silly or wrong, urged to hurry up and feel better. Sometimes we were sent away (time-out) or punished. Our feelings made everyone uncomfortable, and we got the message they weren't welcome.

So when our own kids cry, yell or hit-the-floor in a tantrum, emotions that we buried can get triggered, and we unintentionally pass this invalidation on down to our kids.

(And, by the way, that's my only explanation for the popularity of comedy sites focusing on crying toddlers. Like abuse victims who are compelled to become abusers themselves, the fans of these sites seem to feel giddily empowered ridiculing the vulnerabilities of small children.)

The way most of us diminish feelings is far more subtle and loving. We don't ever want to see our kids hurt or upset, so we try to calm them down by reassuring them, "It's okay," "You're fine," or "It's just a..." But these responses also invalidate, because when children are upset they don't *feel* fine, and our words can't change that. Our 'comforting' responses are confusing, diminishing, teach children not trust their feelings and maybe even to fear them.

One thing in life is certain: Our kids are going to get their feelings hurt. A lot. They'll get rejected by friends, not make the A-team, lose the debate, do poorly on a test and get their hearts broken. Such is life. And it will take every bit of our strength to zip our lips, bite our tongues, just listen, nod, and acknowledge, "That was hurtful." Of course, what we really want to do is shout, "They didn't deserve you!" "You'll do better next time!"

The healthiest message children can get from us is that their darkest moods and harshest feelings will be heard, accepted and understood by us, even when these feelings are about us. Fostering a close lifelong bond with our kids is as simple as that.

30.

The Parent I Might Have Been

Just listen to your instincts... Don't over think and overcomplicate... Every child is different... I often hear these reasons for not embracing a particular parenting approach, and I generally agree. Yet it is hard for me to imagine raising my three children without the gift of clarity I received twenty years ago from Magda Gerber.

Gerber's RIE methods didn't come to me naturally, yet they felt right. She helped me clear away my confusion and focus on what matters most: *real* quality time and the kind of experiences we gain from engaging with our babies as whole people from birth.

Magda gave me tools to recognize the unique perspectives of each of my children, inspiring me to trust their growth, allowing them to develop as individuals, each with a strong sense of self. Her lessons have been completely transformative in terms of my perceptions about babies, children, parenting and life itself. Twenty years later, it has become impossible for me to imagine the parent I might have been without them.

It's also tough to remember how uncomfortable, sometimes even painful it was to learn and adjust to new modes of thought and behavior – like remembering to slow down and talk to a baby even though conventional wisdom tells you he or she doesn't understand.

For all those reasons and more, I've appreciated my correspondence with Emilia Poprawa from Poland. Her learning experiences as she applies Magda's Educaring Approach are like a mirror of my own development, and perhaps thousands of other parents worldwide.

Emilia agreed to allow me to share two of her letters. The first reminds me of the passion I felt as a new parent to 'do it right':

Dear Janet,

I feel very passionate about what I am learning but also somewhat overwhelmed. Perhaps I've found myself in a state of disequilibrium where all I previously assumed about child development is somewhat falling apart, leaving a space for a new paradigm to emerge. It is certainly not easy to change our old ways in favor of new, more effective and compassionate responses.

Slowing down, being present and gentle is by all means not an easy task. I have been trying to cultivate RIE principles in all my affairs but sometimes I feel just stuck in my old ways (when I rush, hurry, and mindlessly move through a day). My hands, instead of conveying a message of calm, sensitivity and patience, are channelling my inner anxiety, mindlessness, and hurry... My mother was a very anxious caregiver. She always rushed and was never truly present. Her hands were rough, irritated and impatient. I see the shadow of her in myself when care for my son.

I have to remind myself that change is frequently a painful process, and as a Zen teacher Shunryu Suzuki said, "In the beginner's mind there are many possibilities, but in the expert's there are few." So with my heart and mind open and hopeful, I take a deep breath and try again to be more present and gentle."

Emilia's subsequent letter is an affirmation of the priceless benefits of Magda's philosophy. It is also a reminder to me -- not of the parent I was, but of the parent I might have been.

Janet,

It has been almost a year since I welcomed my son into this world. It has been almost a year since I welcomed RIE into my life as a parent and caregiver. Needless to say I am grateful and lucky to have a proven roadmap to raise my son.

Proven formula: miracle love + RIE = self-confident baby.

I am not saying that things are always easy and superb. There are many bumps on the road in forms of struggle, frustrations, not knowing, but I found myself always regaining equilibrium, learning from my mistakes and moving on. If I had never come across RIE, this is what my parenting would have been like:

- I would do everything in my power to stop my child from crying, not knowing the importance and meaning of crying.

- I would distract, redirect or use other means to prevent my child from feeling any frustration.

- I would feel that my obligation as a parent is to provide non-stop entertainment for my child and to teach her how things work.

- I would prop him to sit, help him to walk, teach him how to move.

- I would swoop him up without even considering telling him what would happen.

- I would spend lots of money on so-called educational toys.

- I would see my child as helpless little person.

- I would rush through care giving routines to get the job done.

- I would fail to see my son as an initiator and competent explorer with a mind of his own.

- I would still be a loving and devoted mother but more exhausted, depleted and definitely less respectful.

Thank you and all the folks who are working so diligently on promoting the Educaring Approach. I know that it has made a big difference in lives of many families and it made a huge impact on my life!

With love -- Emilia

Thanks

To Mike, my dashing husband, uber-talented editor, publisher, devoted co-parent and so much more. This book was your idea and could not have happened without your enthusiasm, determination and focus.

To Magda Gerber, for transforming my life with your wisdom and spirit. And to Magda's children, Mayo, Daisy and Bence for continuing to honor me with your tremendous support.

To Lisa Sunbury (RegardingBaby.org) for being my online "other half" and co-pioneer. I could never have survived all the trials, tribulations, triumphs and trolls without you.

To the RIE Board of Directors, especially Carol Pinto, Polly Elam, and Ruth Money, for your inspiration, mentorship and unwavering support.

To my wise and passionate RIE Associates for your inspiration and collaboration.

To all my associates, fellow bloggers and ECE enthusiasts in the online world. Thank you for teaching and encouraging me. I am especially grateful to Deborah Stewart of *Teach Preschool*, Tom Hobson (*Teacher Tom*), Deborah McNelis of *Brain Insights*, Amanda Morgan of *Not Just Cute*, and (again) Lisa Sunbury of *Regarding Baby* for sharing my work when no one else did.

To Charlotte, Madeline and Ben for making my heart soar with pride and gratitude each day. I would be honored to know such amazing people as you, much less parent them. Thank you for teaching me what life is about, and for making me and RIE look incredibly good.

Recommended Reading

Your Self-Confident Baby, Magda Gerber, Allison Johnson. Published by John Wiley & Sons, Inc. (1998)

Dear Parent – Caring for Infants with Respect, Magda Gerber. Published by Resources for Infant Educarers (2002)

Peaceful Babies – Contented Mothers, Dr. Emmi Pikler. Published by Medicine Press (1971)

Respecting Babies – A New Look at Magda Gerber's RIE Approach, Ruth Anne Hammond, M.A. Published by Zero to Three (2009)

Education for A New World, Maria Montessori. Published by Kalakshetra Publications (1969)

Endangered Minds, Jane M. Healy, Ph.D. Published by Touchstone (1990)

1,2,3… The Toddler Years, Irene Van der Zande

Siblings Without Rivalry, Adele Faber & Elaine Mazlish, Published by W.W. Norton & Co (2012)

How To Talk So Kids Will Listen & Listen So Kids Will Talk, Adele Faber & Elaine Mazlish, Published by Avon Books (1980)

Raising Your Spirited Child, Mary Sheedy Kurcinka, Published by HarperCollins (2012)

The Whole-Brained Child, Daniel J. Seigel, Tina Payne Bryson. Published by Bantam Books (2012)

Becoming The Parent You Want to Be, Laura Davis & Janis Keyser, Published by Broadway Books (1992)

Brain Rules For Babies, John Medina, Published by Pear Press (2014)

Calms - A Guide To Soothing Your Baby, Carrie Contey PhD & Debby Takikawa, Amazon

Mind In The Making, Ellen Galinsky, Published by HarperCollins (2010)

"How Babies Think", Alison Gopnik. *Psychology* (July, 2010)

Made in the USA
San Bernardino, CA
31 July 2015